Teaching From the Thinking Heart

The Practice of Holistic Education

Clive
Thank you
for coming
all best wishes

[signature]

Teaching From the Thinking Heart

The Practice of Holistic Education

edited by

John P. Miller
University of Toronto

Michèle Irwin
University of Toronto

Kelli Nigh
University of Toronto

INFORMATION AGE PUBLISHING, INC.
Charlotte, NC • www.infoagepub.com

Library of Congress Cataloging-in-Publication Data

A CIP record for this book is available from the Library of Congress
http://www.loc.gov

ISBN: 978-1-62396-723-9 (Paperback)
       978-1-62396-724-6 (Hardcover)
       978-1-62396-725-3 (ebook)

Printed in the United States of America

CONTENTS

SECTION II

HOLISTIC PEDAGOGY

PREFACE

Public education with its emphasis on high-stakes testing and competition has a grim, Darwinian feel. In this environment one can ask the question: Is it possible to teach holistically? The papers in this book demonstrate how teachers can engage the whole student, i.e., the head, hands, and the heart; these teachers work from the "thinking heart," a place of wisdom and compassion. Even though the challenges are immense, they show it is also possible to teach with love and joy.

As someone who has been involved in the field of humanistic/holistic education for almost 40 years, I am very excited about this book as it presents the voices of 22 teachers who are engaged in the practice of holistic education. The papers come from a graduate course I teach at the Ontario Institute for Studies in Education at the University of Toronto entitled *The Holistic Curriculum*. Most of the papers come from two sections of the course taught in the summer of 2012. This is a rich and diverse collection of papers showing how holistic education can be brought into public education despite the pressures of testing and accountability measures. Although most of the teachers teach in public schools, there are also examples from teachers working in private and postsecondary settings. I believe this book can inspire other teachers who are looking for ways to teach the whole person in a more connected manner. There are very few texts in the field of holistic education that include the *voices and practices* of teachers, particularly those working in public schools. Many of the examples of holistic education in practice come from Waldorf, Montessori, Reggio Emilia, and alternative schools. A unique feature of this book is the many different voices of

Teaching From the Thinking Heart, pages xi–xii
Copyright © 2014 by Information Age Publishing
All rights of reproduction in any form reserved.

teachers describing their work in the classroom; they talk about their successes, the challenges, and even a few failures.

Another unique feature of the book is the diversity of perspectives. Toronto has been identified as one of the most multicultural cities in the world and the classes at OISE reflect this diversity. Most students in the course come from Canada, but other students whose papers are included in the book came from the following countries: Chile, Egypt, and Kenya. Some of the papers describe the relevance of holistic education in these contexts.

In the introductory chapter I discusses in detail the pedagogy that I employ throughout the course. The course itself is based on holistic learning principles and covers the theory and practice of holistic education and includes a requirement that students meditate every day for 6 weeks (4½ in the summer session). The rest of the book then includes papers from teachers that focus on examples of holistic practices, holistic pedagogy, and teacher narratives. In the last chapter my coeditors, Michèle Irwin and Kelli Nigh, identify some of the major themes in the book.

I draw inspiration from my students, most of whom teach in public schools in Southern Ontario. I first started teaching The Holistic Curriculum in 1985, and since then I have taught over 2,000 students in this course. The papers in this book show how it is possible to make a real difference in public education despite the current environment. It is my hope that this book will inspire many more teachers to teach from the thinking heart.

—**John P. Miller**

ACKNOWLEDGMENTS

I am grateful to each teacher who contributed a chapter to this book. When I first read these papers in my course The Holistic Curriculum, I was moved and inspired. In scholarly publications it is rare to hear the voice of the teacher. I urge the reader to listen to these voices with hope that they too can be inspired. There are also many teachers who have been in my courses over the past thirty years whose work could not be included here. However, they too helped me recognize the importance of editing a book that includes the teacher's voice in holistic education.

The book would not have been possible without the work of my co-editors, Michèle Irwin and Kelli Nigh. They worked with the contributors, honoring their effort and refining their words into publishable form. Thank you, Michèle and Kelli.

I want to thank Nel Noddngs, who wrote the book's Foreword. Nel's important work was recently celebrated in the book, *Dear Nel*, and I am deeply appreciative of her support for this project.

I must also express gratitude to my institution, The Ontario Institute for Studies in Education at the University of Toronto, and particularly my department, Curriculum, Teaching and Learning (CTL). I have worked at OISE for over forty years. The department and my colleagues in CTL have supported my work in holistic education and helped make this book possible.

Finally, I am grateful to George Johnson and the staff at IAP. Information Age Publishing has published three books that I have either co-edited or written, and two of these books, *Transcendental Learning: The Educational Legacy of Alcott, Emerson, Fuller, Peabody and Thoreau* and *Teaching from the Thinking Heart: The Practice of Holistic Education*, have personal significance for me. Emerson, in his essay on education, wrote about "methods of love" in teaching, and I believe that the teachers in this book show how such methods are central to the practice of holistic education.

—John P. Miller

CHAPTER 1

TEACHING FROM THE THINKING HEART

The Practice of Holistic Education

John P. Miller
University of Toronto

INTRODUCTION

I do my best to facilitate the creation of conditions where students' souls are safe and acknowledged, through building a healthy classroom community and recognizing the whole student. Let us share our souls. Let the real learning begin.

—Julia Verhaeghe

Julia, a teacher and a student in my Holistic Curriculum class in the summer of 2012, wrote this in her paper in my class. Holistic education seeks what Julia calls "real learning" that engages the whole person—body, mind, and soul. In this book 22 teachers describe their efforts to facilitate real learning. They also share their souls and how they teach from the "thinking heart" (Wex, 2009, p. 143). To me, the thinking heart means teaching with wisdom and compassion. I think you will find that the teachers in this collection teach from this place, which is also a place of humility. They acknowledge the challenges and difficulties of doing this in public school classrooms, yet these papers are examples of how holistic education can be practiced successfully in a variety of settings. Besides public and private schools in Canada, there are also descriptions of teaching the deaf in Chile, and teaching English in a technical institute in an Arab country in the Arabian/Persian gulf.

In 1985, I began teaching a graduate course entitled *The Holistic Curriculum*. I have taught this course almost every year since then at the Ontario Institute for Studies in Education at the University of Toronto. Most of the students are experienced teachers working on a master's degree. In the summer of 2012, I taught two sections of the course, and the student papers were among the best I have read. This book is a collection of those papers. Since they have been written by teachers, these papers are outstanding examples of how holistic education can be brought into public school classrooms at the elementary and secondary levels. A few of the teachers worked in private schools and in post-secondary settings.

In this introductory chapter, I will outline the basic concepts that are presented in the course to provide the context for reading the papers. I first describe the concepts and then some of the teaching methods that I use in the class. As much as possible, the class attempts to employ holistic learning principles. This chapter presents the concepts in the sequence that I use in the course.

HOLISTIC EDUCATION

Holistic education has two important dimensions. First, it focuses on growth of the whole person—body, mind, and soul. It acknowledges that within the human psyche there is an aspect which is unknowable and irreducible. The term that I use to describe this part of human experience is *soul* (Moore, 1992; Miller, 2000). Soul is defined as a mysterious energy that gives meaning and purpose to life. Holistic education differs from most other forms of pedagogy because it includes the spiritual dimension. Gandhi wrote that body, mind, and soul form an indivisible whole and that it is a gross fallacy to focus on only one aspect (e.g., the mind). Holistic education, then, engages the whole person.

The second dimension is the focus on the *interconnectedness* between experience and the surrounding environment. Both the scientist and the mystic have developed a picture of reality that indicates a deep interconnectedness. From science we know that a minor change in an ecosystem can lead to changes throughout the system. Spiritual teachers have also shared this insight. The ancient Chinese teacher Lao-tse had the vision and said all things were connected through the Tao. The Suquamish Indian, Chief Seattle, on his deathbed, said: "All things are connected like the blood which unites one family." Holistic Education attempts to be congruent with nature

The second reflection is by Rebecca Ryder, who was pregnant during the course.

My experience with bringing meditation into my life over the past month has been really amazing. I can't believe how much my body and mind were able to learn about such a practice in just four weeks. I was consistent with my practice, meditating nearly every day over the course of the month, and I found it incredible to watch the changes happen along the way. Sometimes I noticed an improvement in what I was capable of doing from day to day. That's not to say it has been easy. Other times, I found it very challenging, and I experienced a few frustrating days when I seemed to regress with my practice. Just as I felt like I was getting "good" at my meditation, I would have a session in which I would be completely distracted or full of thoughts. I suppose that's all part of being a beginner and learning the practice. The great news is that these frustrating and challenging moments came less frequently as I grew more comfortable with my practice.

It's amazing how hard it is to "be." I suppose it's so different from what I'm used to doing in my head; creating the never-ending 'to do' list, debating and making critical decisions about daily tasks (like what to make for dinner) and wondering about what he thinks and what she thinks and why. After nearly a month of practice it feels like a gift, like a luxury to have this fifteen minutes every day as a break from those endless thoughts. I have noticed that my mind is a bit calmer, not just during the meditation but also at different moments throughout the day. I have been waking up with less anxiety about what I have to get done throughout the day and the horribly sad and scary dreams that I was having during the first trimester of my pregnancy have subsided a bit. After my meditation, I often feel calmer, stronger, more energized and more in-control. For me, the most wonderful thing about my daily meditation is that it's a time for me to be completely aware of my pregnancy and connect with my baby. Often the days are so busy that I reach the evening without having noticed or given thought to anything about this incredible time in my life except for a pain in my back or the discomfort of indigestion. During my meditation I take time to send positive thoughts and energy to my baby and really appreciate this special time. I feel more connected to my pregnancy because of it.

I wrote in my journal recently that I feel lucky to have been introduced to this practice and that it is becoming a part of my life. My intention is to continue with my practice throughout my pregnancy and beyond. I'm sure it will have incredible benefits when life becomes hectic for different reasons, as a new parent.

One woman, who was in my class about three years ago, sent me an e-mail with pictures of her new born twins. She wrote that focusing on her breathing was helpful in giving birth.

CONCLUSION

Toronto has been identified as one of the most multicultural cities in the world. My classes reflected this diversity. Of course, most students came from Canada, but others in the two classes came from the following countries: Chile, China, Egypt, India, Italy, Kenya, Turkey, and the Ukraine. Some of the papers describe their experience in these countries. Students from these different places could see the relevance of holistic education to their own context. They also came from almost all the major faith traditions and found the meditation practice was helpful.

So much of educational dialogue today emphasizes competition and test results. These papers show there is another way that is deeply organic and demonstrates how education can nourish the whole child. As you read the papers, I hope you can feel the passion, joy and commitment that these teachers share in their work. I did when I read them last summer and felt that had to be shared with a larger audience. My hope is that their work can inspire other teachers to work from a holistic perspective that recognizes the beauty of mystery in each child.

Maria Karmiris works with children with special needs. I found her writing about this work very moving. She ends her paper with what teaching from the thinking heart means to her:

> I am aware as well that the moments of greatest significance to me do not revolve around any of the content, facts, strategies that I have taught. What I remember most are those moments of connection. What all these moments seem to have in common is being present, being in awe and wonder, being open to changing your mind and feeling an overwhelming sense of loving-kindness. This is what teaching with heart means to me. I remain unsure if anything I have done has had a transformative effect on my students. I know for sure my time connecting with my students has transformed me.

REFERENCES

Abram, D. (1996). *The spell of the sensuous.* New York: Vintage.

Drake, S. M., Bebbington, J., Laksman, D., Mackie, P., Maynes, N., & Wayne, L. (1992). *Developing integrated curriculum using the story model.* Toronto: OISE Press.

Drake, S. (1998). *Creating integrated curriculum.* Thousand Oaks, CA: Corwin.

Emerson, R. W. (2003). *Selected writings.* New York: Signet.

Gibbs, J. (1987). *Tribes: A process for social development and cooperative learning.* Santa Rosa, CA: Center Source Publications.

Johnson, R. T., & Johnson, D. W. (1994). An overview of cooperative learning. In J. Thousand, A. Villa, & A. Nevin, (Eds.) *Creativity and collaborative learning.* (pp.1–23) Baltimore: Brookes Press.

Kiefer, J., & Kemple, M. (1998) *Digging deeper: Integrating youth gardens into schools & communities.* Montpelier, VT.: Common Roots Press.

King, M. L. (1968, May) *Negro history bulletin. 31*(12).

Lin, J. (2006). *Love, peace and wisdom in education: A vision for education in the 21st century.* Lanham, MD: Rowan and Littlefield Education.

McGilchrist, I. (2009). *The master and his emissary: The divided brain and the making of the western world.* New Haven: Yale University Press.

McLuhan, T. C. (1972). *Touch the Earth: A self-portrait of Indian existence.* New York: Pocket Books.

Miller, J. P. (2000). *Education and the soul: Toward a spiritual curriculum.* Albany, NY: SUNY Press.

Miller, J. P., & Nozawa, A. (2002). Meditating teachers: A qualitative study. *Journal of in-service education, 28*(1),179(en}192.

Miller, J. P. (2007). *The holistic curriculum.* Toronto: U. of Toronto Press.

Miller, J. P. (2010). *Whole child education.* Toronto: U. of Toronto Press.

Miller, J. P. (2012). Contemplative practices in teacher education: What I have learned. In L. Groen, E. Coholic, & J. R. Graham (Eds.), *Spirituality in education and social work: An interdisciplinary dialogue.* Waterloo, Ont: Wilfrid Laurier Press.

Moore, T. (1992) *Care of the soul.* New York: Walker.

Moore, T. (2002) *The soul's religion.* New York: Harper Collins.

Neves, A. (2009). *A holistic approach to the Ontario curriculum: Moving to a more coherent curriculum.* MA thesis at the University of Toronto.

Nowak, M. A. (2011). *Super cooperators: Altruism, evolution, and why we need each other to succeed.* New York: Free Press.

Porte, J. (Ed.). (1982). *Emerson in his journals.* Cambridge, MA: Harvard University Press.

Taylor, J. B. (2009). *My stroke of insight: A brain scientist's personal journey.* New York: Plume.

Wex, M. (2009). *How to be a mentsh (& not a shmuck).* Toronto: Knopf

Whitman, W. (1993). *From this soil.* New York: The Nature Co.

SECTION I

EXAMPLES OF HOLISTIC EDUCATION

CHAPTER 2

DEAREST STUDENTS

A Teacher's Letter of Reflection

Nina Moore
University of Toronto

Dearest Students,

I write this letter to you all, my students of the past, present and future. As you may know, I've been teaching a medley of grades at the same school over the last 11 years. This has afforded me the luxury of seeing some of you grow from Kindergarten to Grade 8, and of getting to know your family and community.

When you walk through the classroom door, you are a whole human being. You are a writer/reader/scientist/visual artist/musician/inventor/ researcher. You have wisdom, knowledge, life experience, strong likes and dislikes, interests, relationships, sorrows, joys, multiple identities, and so very many curiosities. I know it may sound silly to some of you for me to explicitly declare this, but most of you already know, that my profession often functions on the ideology that just as we attempt to compartmentalize knowledge, we do the same to you. The education system often insults your intelligence, as well as my own. We tackle education as if it were only

Teaching From the Thinking Heart, pages 21–28

our duty to nurture your academic side and as if your academic identity is somehow isolated from your soul.[1]

* * *

I invest my energy in meeting your needs, which includes fostering your developing independence. It is not my job to "complete" you, nor is it my job to fill you up with facts, for you are not incomplete, nor empty.[2] I have learned that only when I strive to honor your full self, can I expect to witness your full academic potential. To focus only on the former inevitably sends you the message that I am only invested in your short-term success (your next report card, your next test score).

I promise to never misdirect my energy on promotions that inevitably distance myself from your day-to-day realities.

I am weary on your behalf of any "expert" that looks to advise me on what or how you should learn. When they don't take the time to learn about and from you, I will protect you from their top-down agenda.

I will never voluntarily impose any arbitrary criteria on you. I will never keep you from creating and investigating in order to make my assessment strictly standardized and quantifiable. I will never compromise your learning in order to impress my "superiors." When top-down mandated testing is forced on us, I promise to remind you that you are more than a test score. I know that sometimes I take out my frustration about these mandates on you and for that I apologize.

It's been since last September that I've given you a traditional paper and pencil test (apart from board-mandated ones). I have come to a place where only a spelling test at the end of our first month is necessary. It is a spelling test of the names of your classmates and teachers that we have been investigating all month. We have examined patterns, syllables, rhyming words and similarities and differences among them. We have put them in alphabetical order and spelled them out in sign language. During that test, some of you will be working hard to spell our first names, others to write the first letter of every name and some of you will be adding last names. All of you are working hard. Because I have used so many avenues to observe and document your growth, I no longer understand the purpose of the "end of unit" test. In fact, because knowledge is fluid, not linear and fragmented, the "unit" is a concept that I now struggle with. As you know, I love to work with themes which when granted the time, space, and flexibility, unfold organically.[3]

* * *

When I see you as the complex and unique beings that you are, I am better able to meet your needs by using my energy more wisely. For example, instead of corralling you to "get started" first thing each morning, experience and observation have taught me, that like adults, you need to start you day at your own tempo. Some of you may have woken up only fifteen minutes before; some of you haven't stopped rushing since getting up. Whatever the case, I know that getting to school is a challenge. You may be like me, in that you need uninterrupted time to gently rouse yourself into full wakefulness.

I've learned that some of you need to just plop yourself down in your chair, coat and bag still on, for a good few minutes. Some among you need to stand at the chalkboard to read and absorb our daily outline even before your first social interaction. Some of you go about your own routine independently or with a cherished classmate (checking on plants, perusing a book, updating the calendar). I know that some of you need your snack immediately before you are able to fully concentrate. Some of you need to start your day with a trip to the washroom and some of you need to neatly arrange and take inventory of your very own treasured school supplies. Some of you are already working away, oblivious to the happenings in our classroom. Some of you are moody, depressed, or anxious. Others are content, joyful, even excited. I've come to understand that some of you need to check-in with me first thing, while others aren't yet ready for adult interaction.

I will never embarrass or scold you for being late. I can already see it on your face that you hate arriving after the bell. I will wish you a good morning and give you some time to quietly get settled in, just like your peers have already done.

I have learned that it is my responsibility to nurture a classroom culture that supports and respects all of these needs. You have taught me that when I am patient enough to allow the above to occur, you respond with increased engagement. I must tell you that some of my happiest moments in our classroom have been while sipping my coffee and observing this whole process unfold. Some mornings when we start with our writing workshop, you are so fully engrossed that the recess bell interrupts our writing, editing, mini lessons, conferencing or sharing to the class. It is at these times that I feel that I am having an impact on your intrinsic love of learning and hard work.[4]

——*

Our classroom walls have sections painted blue and green as I simply can't stand staring at dirty unkempt walls and I don't think you should have to either. I chose blue and green because they are soothing colors, and I find them aesthetically pleasing as well. I strive to create for you an environment that will foster your creativity, curiosity and sense of belonging.[5] I think that it is important to let you start with a blank canvas, in that I try not to fill your walls and shelves with information and pictures before you even walk through the door in September. Instead, we build our unique collection of knowledge. If your writing, for example, demonstrates that you are ready to use alternatives to the word "said," we brainstorm and research new options and then post them for future reference. Our walls reflect your learning and they should include your printing as well as mine.

As we collect data, develop new skills, and ask increasingly complex questions, I think that it is important to post evidence of this on our walls for future referencing and editing.

*   *   *

In September, before our first big clean up, we meet on the carpet to brainstorm what needs to happen in order for an efficient and thorough clean up to occur. I document this for us on chart paper. We keep it posted and meet to revise it as needed. After a while, I can take it down and tuck it away. If we are getting rusty with our clean up routine, I'll bring it out so that we can review and revise it. You have taught me that this is much more meaningful than having me state the clean up rules at the beginning of the year.[6]

*   *   *

I always have at least a hundred library books borrowed at a time and I hope that this helps you to remember that the library is a valuable tool. I know that some of you really enjoy keeping our book bins in order and constantly changing their themes. Your help is greatly appreciated because it allows me more time for you and your classmates, and it helps me to stay in touch with your current interests. I love it when you display library books and your handmade books around the classroom for others to learn from. Sometimes I read to you, sometimes you read to me. Sometimes you read by yourself and so do I. Thank you for all the lovely class books you have made over the years, which inspire and encourage the students after you.

*   *   *

I like to think that I provide you with many choices, but you've taught me that it takes a lot of time, structure, and routine to create a safe and calm space where you can function within a framework that is based on choice and independence. Contrary to what some educators may assume, we, as a class, have developed routines and procedures for countless situations. We have come to know who is good at fixing the stapler, who can help you with spelling or sketching you a picture. Gradually, I witness you increasingly do this without needing to consult me or interrupt your classmates unnecessarily. Because of this, you allow me to work with small groups or individuals.

Truthfully, Septembers can really test my patience because I am eager to look around our classroom and see every single one of you engaged in an activity of your choice, but you teach me patience and show me that this is an unfair expectation if I do not provide the proper scaffolding.

In pink letters I've posted *PATIENCE* at the front of the room. I reference it all the time, sometimes silently and sometimes aloud. I do my best to remind you to be patient with each other, with me, and especially with yourselves. Aloud, I remind myself that I need patience and understanding as well when I am not feeling listened to by you.

I have noticed that when you know you have many choices, you are more likely to become more absorbed into your learning. For example, I notice that you start taking out clipboards at recess or on the school bus to conduct surveys or document what you see. Projects and books and practice sheets that you have created at home start showing up on my desk.

* * *

Thank you for teaching me about the different ways that you learn. As the social beings that you are, I have discovered that some of you simply need to talk in order to solidify your learning. I have noticed that you need to read the questions to me and then put them into your own words out loud as you look at me not for further instruction but rather only for eye contact.

Thank you for teaching me to listen without interrupting you. I have also noticed, for example, that some of you need to talk through your writing process, from developing plot to self-correcting your spelling. I understand now that you need to share your work in progress with someone you trust who will listen, encourage, and challenge you.[7]

I see too that you may need to stretch out on the carpet or stand while using a waist-high bookshelf as your workspace. I noticed as well that the soothing motion of the rocking chair keeps some of you focused. Sometimes you need to work in the hallway or at my desk.

* * *

Thank you for reminding me every year that a class is a supremely unique entity. You have provided me with countless examples. I remember one year we sang "Don't Worry Be Happy" by Bobby McFerrin at our Winter Concert. Not only that but whenever I popped in the CD, we would all sing along as we did our work. However, the next September when I hit play ready to enjoy another year of bopping along to the beat, you had me turn it off after 30 seconds. You hated it!

Thank you for seeing me a whole person as well. Over the years, I have learned that not only is it safe, but also important to share my flaws. I am no longer preoccupied with keeping a tidy desk in order to model this for you. I have learned that I function well amid organized chaos and that I need to accept that some of you do as well. I am notorious for having dirty coffee cups all over the classroom. You often help me to locate the mug with my current cup of hot coffee. Some of you even wash the scattered ones because you know that otherwise they will collect mold until June.

I always know who has an extra pen when I can't find one. Although I try to bring a healthy lunch to school and have you see me snack on fruit, I also know that you don't judge me when I have to pop across the street for greasy pizza. Thank you for accepting that I don't have a musical bone in my body and that it will be up to those of you who do to choreograph our concert performances. Your comic relief is fantastic, as well. When I was late one day, I will never forget how one of you promptly wrote me a late slip and then went right back to work.

So, as another school year approaches, I wonder who you will be and how we will grow as individuals and as a group. Thank you for the memories from the past and for those yet to come.

With warmth and respect,

Ms. Moore

P.S. Thank you, dear students, for the daily belly laughs. They are the perfect antidote for a teacher's struggles.

AUTHOR'S REFLECTION

As I reread this piece, written a couple of years ago, I couldn't help but feel like a fraud. My most recent year of teaching hadn't looked or felt like this at all. Sometimes I had, in fact, corralled my students to get started in the morning. I had often looked around the class and felt frustrated that so many of my students had not been on task. I had often felt overwhelmed as I struggled once again with the dichotomy of my teaching philosophy and board demands.

Upon reflection, however, I see now that some years are easier than others to maintain my integrity and sense of impact. Whether it is due to politics, my own life, the chemistry among my students, or likely some combination thereof, each day, month, or school year has the potential to make me feel like a brand new teacher or an experienced wise one.

NOTES

1. Dr. John P. Miller believes that engaging the soul is a fundamental part of a holistic curriculum. "The soul opens to us when we are . . . deeply involved in our work" (p. 14). When our students are fully engaged, learning is meaningful and complex, which inevitably leads to academic curiosity and success.
2. Dr. Maria Montessori believed that "our intervention in this marvelous process [of teaching] is indirect; we are here to offer to this life, which came into the world by itself, the means necessary for its development and having done that we must await this development with respect" (1965 p. 134). Our role, as teachers, is to guide and support students in their own discovery and creation of knowledge.
3. Dr. Miller (2007) notes "unfortunately, the human world since the Industrial Revolution has stressed compartmentalization and standardization. The result has been fragmentation." This mentality is echoed in the way our curriculum looks at knowledge. Counter to holistic education, distinct subjects make it difficult for many students to connect learning to their own lives. However, described as the "transformation position" by Dr. Miller, its approach "acknowledges the wholeness of the child" (p. 11). When learning is approached by theme rather than specific curriculum expectations, a student can inquire and connect new learning to her interests and her own life.
4. The Reggio Emilia Approach to early childhood education values "fluid and elastic" scheduling (Wurm, 2005, p. 53). There are no bells in Reggio schools. Jullianne P. Wurm, author of Working in the Reggio Way, explains that although young students can expect the same series of activities in a predictable order, the flow is not dictated by a clock but rather by the learners. This approach reminds me to disengage from the culture of minute-to-minute scheduling bestowed on my students and me. To constantly have to pack up and change directions hinders deep, meaningful learning.
5. The Reggio Approach inspired me to carefully reconsider the environment in which my students learn. Why is it that they have to stand on a chair to get a good look out the window? Why do these windows require the strength of an adult to open and close them?

    Although I cannot change the permanent fixtures of a classroom, the Reggio Approach reminds me to step back and let the students lead. Wurm observed that Reggio classrooms "did not jump out at the children but instead offered a place for the students to hang their experience. She explains that, "the classroom served as a canvas upon which the students and teachers could create their own body of work"(p. 31).
6. I do struggle with the fine line between chaos and chaotic order. However, Dr. Herbert R. Kohl inspires me to take the risk. He said, "The first day is not filled with the mastery of routines and the pronouncement of rules. It is not possible to anticipate which rules and routines will emerge as convenient or necessary for a particular class" (1969, p. 29). Dr. Kohl reminds us that the purpose of rules is to facilitate the functioning of a classroom and the well-being of each person.

7. A "delicate intervention" (p. 131) is how Dr. Montessori described the process of us supporting our students. She explained that we are to "guide the child so that [we] may be always ready to supply the desired help, but may never be the obstacle between the child and [her] experience" (p. 131, 1965). Dr. Montessori reminds me that sometimes there is no need for intervention. "'Wait while observing.' That is the motto for the educator" (p. 132).

REFERENCES

Kohl, H. B. (1969). *The open classroom*. New York, NY: The New York Review.

Miller, J. P. (2007). *The holistic curriculum* (2nd ed.). Toronto, ON: OISE Press.

Montessori, M. (1965). *Dr. Montessori's own handbook: A short guide to her ideas and materials*. New York, NY: Schocken Books Inc.

Wurm, J. P. (2005). *Working the Reggio way: A beginner's guide for American teachers*. St. Paul, MN: Redleaf Press.

CHAPTER 3

HOLISTIC TEACHING IN THE AFTER SCHOOL COOKING CLUB

Dan Gullery
University of Toronto

A good friend of mine once told me something about bell peppers that stayed with me. She said that you could tell a lot about a person by the type of pepper they choose to serve stuffed, especially at a dinner party. The least desirable choice would be green bell peppers, as they are the least expensive and most commonly found. Choosing to serve stuffed green peppers shows a lack of: motivation, experience in the kitchen, and care for your guests. Next on the list are orange, red, and yellow bell peppers. These are usually just as common as green peppers, but often a little bit more expensive. Choosing one of these shows a level of sophistication and care for your guests, but still suggests you are unsure of yourself and not willing to take risks. Finally, there is the choice of any other type of pepper, whether poblanos, purple bell peppers, habañeros, or any other exotic variety. Choosing one of these peppers shows that you've taken the time and effort to go out of your way to find something unique, and that you've put thought and care into preparing this meal and catering to your guests. While the stuffing

Teaching From the Thinking Heart, pages 29–36

itself is also of great importance, the peppers themselves carry great weight and significance. This simple explanation somehow struck a chord with me, and I haven't served stuffed green bell peppers since.

Holistic education is, in many ways, a lot like choosing, preparing, and serving stuffed peppers at a dinner party. The choices we make in selecting the peppers we'll be using speak volumes to our devotion and care. If we want to teach holistically, we must recognize the framework and the content as equally important. We must recognize our students as guests in our rooms who deserve to be nourished and fulfilled. Not with common and simplistic tools, but with care, devotion, and skill. Our students deserve to leave our classrooms feeling more satisfied than they were when they originally entered.

Flash forward to my second year of full-time teaching. Towards the middle of the month of November, we had a long staff meeting where we questioned the lack of student involvement in the school. What was going on here? Why were the students so uninvolved and disengaged? The consensus, after much discussion, seemed to be that students did not feel they really had a space to gather and that the teachers were not offering activities that students were genuinely interested in. The principal offered her full support to any teacher who wanted to form a new activity for students. I knew that somewhere, in the neglected depths of the school, was a long-forgotten home economics room that was currently used as storage, but still equipped with four working ovens, a mass of pots, pans, utensils, blenders, etc. And so I offered my time and devotion to starting a cooking club.

Eating is one of the most important activities in our daily lives, yet we are so far removed from our food that we cannot fully comprehend its significance:

> The products of nature and agriculture have been made, to all appearances, the products of industry. Both eater and eaten are thus in exile from biological reality. And the result is a kind of solitude, unprecedented in human experience, in which the eater may think of eating as, first, a purely commercial transaction between him and a supplier and then as a purely appetitive transaction between him and his food. (Berry, 1990, "The pleasure of eating")

By cooking and eating whole foods together in school, there is a chance that students will leave with a more holistic and compassionate understanding of the world and of themselves.

The following morning, I asked my homeroom grade ten students whether anyone would be interested in joining a cooking club. A few of them seemed generally interested, but I didn't see too much of an overwhelming reaction from them. I went ahead with my plans anyway. After some negotiating and planning with the administration, I was granted a practically unlimited budget, as most of the money for student funds hadn't yet been used for the year, and there was no sign of it going anywhere any time soon. So I got down to cleaning. I found a few students who were willing to help me clean out the home economics room in time for us to start cooking club when we returned from December holiday break. We scrubbed every surface, washed every pot, pan, and utensil, relined the shelves, and cleaned out the refrigerators and ovens. Really, in hindsight, this should have been part of the official activity of the cooking club, as taking care of one's space and belongings is phenomenally important in the kitchen.

I will never forget that Tuesday afternoon in the beginning of January, waiting in the home economics room with Mr. C, the other teacher who volunteered to help with the club, and watching in awe as 62 students showed up for cooking club (in a school of only about 250 students)! They piled in, cramming themselves, their jackets and their bags into the room. Both Mr. C and I were equally terrified and ecstatic.

We didn't have enough chickpeas, tahini, or pita to make hummus for everyone. Nor did we have enough ingredients to make a salad for that many people. We did what we could the first day, and then decided to divide up the cooking club into three sections by age range. We met twice a week on a rotating schedule. At first it was only Mr. C and myself, but over the course of the months five other teachers got involved with the club. It seemed that we had somehow, on a whim, created something that brought the school together to do something beautiful and creative (while also being useful and healthy).

Seeing my students outside of the normal classroom setting, bringing their knowledge of food and culture into view, using their hands, laughing and talking while preparing AND eating brought so much joy to my life and the life of the school. This joy quickly developed into an inclusive and holistic learning environment.

COOKING AND THE THREE CURRICULUM ORIENTATIONS

The Recipe: Roasted Red Peppers

> In transmission learning the student acquires and accumulates knowledge and skills. Learning in this form can occur by reading a text or listening to a teacher's explanation. (Miller, 2007, p. 10)

Turn the broiler on the low setting. Grease a baking sheet lightly with olive oil. Using your hands, rub each pepper with a coating of olive oil and place on the baking sheet. Be sure to leave room between the peppers. Place the sheet in the oven on the middle rack. Every 10 or 15 minutes, using a pair of tongs, turn each pepper over. After about an hour, the skins of the peppers will be black on all sides. Take them out of the oven, place them into a bowl and cover it with plastic wrap. Let them steam for 10 or 15 minutes. Remove them from the bowl, carefully remove the skins, and voilà! You have roasted red peppers.

There's something special about the smell of roasted peppers. It reminds you of home, comfort, and warmth. They aren't ready to be used yet, but the aroma of the peppers is in the air and it's adding to the buzz in the room, constantly reminding us of the benefits we will eventually reap from this hard work- the peppers will both be blended into the tomato sauce and sliced atop the salad.

The room is divided into "stations." I'd encouraged students to move around between the stations, rather than staying in one place the whole time, but most of them seemed to settle down in one place and stay put. Still, instructions were left at each station, and Mr. C and I circulated the room to demonstrate how to successfully pull off each of these seemingly simple tasks:

- Removing the garlic peel is one of the most infuriating and intolerable tasks if you don't crush the cloves with a knife first.
- Chopping an onion into even pieces is nearly impossible without first crosscutting and carefully slicing.

As we moved around the room to clarify and demonstrate these things, I was reminded of the significance of these simple explanations in terms of my role as an educator. Although these tasks might seem artless and unassuming, the tricks that people use in the kitchen are generations old, exclusive to cultures and borders (or sometimes they're practically universal). They are meaningful, sacred, and revered. These are not only skills we use and learn to bring ourselves joy and ease of life. They are learned so that we may pass down the stories of our food, the importance of tradition and culture, and, most importantly, the smiles and joys that these foods bring.

As I impart this knowledge to my students, I remember my mother teaching me these same skills, and telling me that it was her father who taught them to her. I wonder first how these students have made it so close to adulthood without being trained in these ways, and I wonder how I will play into their own narratives as they impart these essential tools onto others later in their lives. This begins the cyclical nature of holistic teaching in the kitchen—as we learn and develop these skills, they become our own to use, to alter, and to communicate to others. The act of transmission as seen in the kitchen is, essentially, the same as it is in the classroom: take the information, find ways to make it relevant to you, and be ready to apply it.

PROBLEM SOLVING BURNT ROASTED RED PEPPERS

The transaction position can be characterized by an emphasis on dialogue between teacher and student . . . The learning is generally seen as rational and capable of intelligent behavior or as a *problem solver.*" (Miller, 2007, p. 11)

Smoke is billowing out of the oven.

"Mr. Gullery! It's smoking!"

Panic ensues.

Although we've read the instructions and carefully applied them to what we're doing, the peppers in this particular oven seem to have burnt too quickly. So, what could have gone wrong? Any number of things, really, but let's assume that it has something to do with the thermometer in the oven.

"It's alright that one side of the peppers burnt. We can still use them. How can we fix this so that the other sides don't burn?"

There is a brief discussion amongst the students, and the consensus is, finally, to lower the tray in the oven for the remainder of the time. The peppers stop burning. My students had taken the information they were given, added some of their own, and solved this problem.

I am circulating around the room and checking in on the various "stations" that have been set up. Some people are peeling and dicing garlic and onions. Others are sauteing the vegetables to add to a tomato sauce. Some students are simply taking a break and chatting. One young man is dutifully scrubbing dishes as they come to him in a steady stream.

I am a little taken aback by the sight of Eric, the football/soccer/hockey/lacrosse playing all-star jock. He is wearing an apron and rubber gloves. Skillfully he scrubs the dishes, stacking them on the drying rack with such precision that it seems he has been born to do this. I ask him very frankly just what is going on. I had assumed that this had been some kind of punishment at the hands of his peers—some kind of retaliation, that he had been *sentenced* to the sink.

"This is what I do. When you live alone with just your mom, and she works two jobs just to be able to pay for you to play sports, get to school, and live a comfortable life, you learn to give back in any way you can."

After about a minute of standing there, awestruck, smiling at him, he starts to laugh.

"It's no big deal, sir! That's just life!"

And he's right. It really is "just life." But seeing this student who, in the past, had driven me crazy with his belligerent misogyny and homophobia, his macho-man attitude and the weight of his physical force, now in such a humble and graceful position, I had no choice but to laugh myself. There was an exchange of information—a transaction—going on between us that never would have found its way out if not for the kitchen.

I approach the "avocado station." Three of my female students are dicing avocados for the salad we're making on the side. One of them, Anna, tells me she'd like to show me how her South American grandmother cuts into avocados. She tells me that it's much easier and more effective than the way I've told them to do it, and that it reminds her of her culture and where the avocados actually come from. As part of this transactional learning, I sit down at the table and watch as she cuts a whole avocado in half with one swift, experienced slice. She picks up the half with the pit still in it, places it in her palm, and, before I can tell her that this probably isn't a good idea, she slams the knife into the pit, twists, and pulls it out. A clean cut. Still, I ask her to please use a spoon to remove the pit while she's at school.

(Weeks later, being the "experienced" chef that I am, I show my partner this wonderful method at home in our own kitchen. I spent the better part of that night in the emergency room, getting five stitches in my finger.)

Roasted Red Peppers and Breaking Bread

> Transformational learning acknowledges the wholeness of the child. The curriculum and child are no longer seen as separate but as connected. (Miller, 2007, p. 11)

There's something eternally beautiful about sitting down at a table and breaking bread together. In every culture throughout history people have seen the act of eating together as a significant ritual. The word "festival" even contains the root word "feast." To sit down and break bread is nourishing for both the body and the soul.

I sat, on many occasions, with my students in the cafeteria while they ate lunch. Sometimes it was when I was on supervision duty, or when I went down to the cafeteria to get something for myself to eat. Other times, I sat in my classroom eating lunch, and left the door open for students who may have found themselves alone to come in to talk and eat. But these were usually minor, coincidental encounters. They ended as quickly as they began, and there was really no mention of the importance of the act of eating. This changed with the communal eating that came with the cooking club. Each time we met, sometimes after more than an hour of prepping and cooking food, washing dishes, and scrubbing surfaces, we all sat down to eat.

Eating food that you've cooked together with your students opens endless doors to conversation. We all have stories surrounding the food we're eating—whether the stories are that this is the first time we have eaten it, that our mothers and grandmothers have prepared similar dishes in the past, or even that we'd never imagined eating something like the food we're eating now. Sharing stories over food is an inescapably joyous occasion, and the stories we shared were exclusively positive—not by instruction, but by default. There is a lack of genuine happiness in schools, and to find a place to experience it is nothing short of a blessing.

I recall one particular student, Christina, telling me while making spaghetti and tomato sauce that she absolutely despised tomatoes and would never eat them. This was an interesting thing to say while she had her hands deep in a bowl of boiled and peeled tomatoes and was feverishly crushing them. I watched as she poured the now-liquid tomatoes in the bowl into the deep saucepan, simmering with onions and garlic. Little swirls of olive oil could still be seen amidst the mass of tomato. I told her that she should at least try the sauce when it was ready, because she had spent so much time and effort preparing it. In the end, she did try it, as she dipped a loaf of Italian bread into a bowl of sauce—her sauce. She sat at the table smiling with her friends and eating this food that she had helped to prepare. I don't know whether she particularly liked it or not, but she ate it and she was happy.

Sitting down to eat with people is a time to share experiences and passions. I probably opened myself up to my students during these meals more than I had at any other time. These were times when we shared mutual stories about love and about life. I told them funny stories from my past about working in restaurants and how these experiences led to my love of working with people and my love of feeding people. I discussed a particular time when, working in a pizzeria as a cashier, I had to fill in for one of the pizza chefs at the last minute and I had to learn, on the spot, how to prepare the dough, shape it into the form of a pizza, put it in the oven, take it back out, and cut and box it, all during a busy lunch rush. Students told me stories about the restaurants that they went to, sometimes the restaurants that were in their families, and their experiences being there, what they learned, and how it helped shape them. In terms of teaching to the whole child, "breaking bread" is perhaps the most opportune time to teach. There is no classroom structure; there is no student/teacher dynamic. There are only people sitting and sharing.

I did notice a shift in my relationship with the students who came to cooking club after we started it. I'm sure this is pretty common in terms of a teacher leading an activity or sport and the students who are participating in it, but it was a unique experience for me. Students who I never dreamed would come to talk to me at lunch or after school started to come by. They wanted to know what I was eating, wanted to show me what they were eating, wanted to share with me the meals that they had cooked at home and impressed their parents with.

In hearing the stories and sharing my own, I am reminded of my friend Tara and her explanation of stuffed peppers. I tried my hardest to bring to this educational setting the most diverse, exotic, and meaningful frameworks to be developed. My students and all of their stories—all of these intricate little details of their lives- these are all their own ingredients that they bring to stuff the peppers. Afterwards, we are left with something more complete than would have been possible without these interactions. This, I think, is holistic education. All of us brought something unique and valuable to the table, and it was only then that we were able to make something beautiful. The three educational orientations: transmission, transaction and transformation, allowed everyone involved in this learning to make connections, find humility, and build new relationships. The content itself was always important, but it was never the finish line. There was an infinite amount of learning that took place beyond that defined end goal, and it was only accessed through these holistic practices.

REFERENCES

Berry, W. (1990). *What are people for?: Essays*. [Kobo file] San Francisco: North Point Press.

Miller, J. P. (2007). *The holistic curriculum*. (2nd ed.). Toronto, ON: University of Toronto Press.

CHAPTER 4

TRIBES

A Transformative Tool
for the 21st Century

Sarah Lowes
University of Toronto

If we understand the school to be a microcosm of society, then changes we wish to see in the world need to be developed, practiced, and felt in our classrooms. We must start by having our students learn harmony, compassion, and respect for one another in a safe environment. It's unfortunate that education has deviated so far from such an innate concept of symbiosis, though it is not surprising given its historical, political, and economic roots. It is now necessary for teachers to unite and teach confidently about the human experience, body, mind, and soul if we want to develop a healthy population and sustainable world moving forward. Empowering ourselves coupled with recognition that we each have a role in shaping the world around us presently and for future generations can be powerful starting points. Spiritual teachers, leading scientific researchers, religious scholars, important public intellectuals, and major writers were interviewed as research for *Living Deeply: The Art & Science of Transformation in Everyday*

Teaching From the Thinking Heart, pages 37–42
Copyright © 2014 by Information Age Publishing
All rights of reproduction in any form reserved.

Life (Schlitz, Vieten, & Amorok, 2007). A thread that transcended the diverse worldviews among interviewees was a "big-picture view of individual growth as part of a larger collective evolution" (p. 96). While consciousness transformation is a personal journey for each individual, a connection to each other, the Earth, and the universe can be fostered in the classroom with open hearts.

Enter Tribes. Tribes is more than a program or collection of activities, as Jeanne Gibbs (2006) describes in *Reaching All by Creating Tribes Learning Community*. While the definitive meaning of Tribes continually evolves, Gibbs describes Tribes as "an ongoing goal-oriented process based on sound principles and practices that maximize academic, social, and emotional development and learning for today's children" (2006, p. x). For me, Tribes is an approach that validates each person for their uniqueness and allows each individual to develop an awareness of the interconnectedness of one's presence and energy, while being inspired to live more harmoniously in the universe. It's a transformational tool that helps educators provide a meaningful educational experience for students in the twenty-first century; an experience they deserve and lack in our current industrial and capitalist focused system. Tribes roots itself in holistic and whole school/child education with strong parallels to many of the values we see being called for by one of the great teachers of our time, Joanna Macy. In *Active Hope: How to face the mess we're in without going crazy* (2012), Macy shares an influential and pivotal recounting of the Shambala Warrior Prophecy from the Tibetan Buddhist tradition. She compellingly describes how compassion and insight can motivate us to recognize the "radical interdependence of all phenomena" (p. 102). Macy further articulates how a collaborative model of power deepens one's sense of community, highlighting the principle that "everyone can play a role and that everyone has something to offer" (p. 130). Both Macy and Gibbs (2006) wish to bring light towards new ways of interacting and being in the world, cultivating respect and collaboration amongst diverse populations. To personally communicate the power of holistic education I would like to share my experience about a transformative year of Teacher's College with a Tribes certified teacher, Gail Phillips. Interestingly, Gail's teacher reflection can be found as a vignette in *Whole Child Education* (Miller, 2010, p. 57), though we discuss different cohorts.

TRIBES: A FOLLOW-UP PERSPECTIVE

After finding a seat in my teacher education program's "homeroom" equivalent (cohorts based upon school board preference), I wondered how the class would engage (or disengage) me. Coming from a competitive, four year undergraduate degree it was a negative question that often presented itself as I sat passively in lecture halls. A group of roughly 30 adults sat quietly awaiting the start of class, a routine that became more comfortable over the year long preservice teacher program. Gail identifies her classroom as a "Tribes" classroom, though this is not outwardly discussed until a couple weeks into our preservice year. I found Teacher's College to be a particularly interesting experience, as an adult student I was studying pedagogy and was given time to reflect and critically engage with the teachings around me. I knew early on that Gail was going to be one of those teachers that altered my educational perspective.

Our first few days of class had little formal "academic" content. We played various name games and ice-breakers, partner introductions, value lines that had us standing on a spectrum based on our beliefs about nutrition, for instance, shared life maps that outlined our journeys thus far, and shared personal photographs. This participation in cooperative games had us laughing and getting to know each other quickly, connecting us as people before anything else. It wasn't long before energy filled the room. Initially, students made it to class at their own leisurely, acceptable pace, though before long people began arriving earlier to have a coffee or tea, a snack, and to converse with their peers. There was always an informal, casual period at the start of the class that helped develop or nourish friendships. A chime of lovely cymbals echoed in the room indicating a more formal start to class, but nonetheless discussions were allowed to finish up.

I watched Gail curiously and diligently to learn how she had created such a harmonious, cooperative environment with such ease. It was more than her direct eye contact and warm smiles, her full attention when conversing with you, or her asking follow-up questions to previous conversations. It was more than her calm and reflective nature, intuition, or willingness to go with the flow of the class. If I had to choose one thing that made the experience so positive, it would be the authenticity with which she cared. Gail and her teaching partners genuinely recognized and cared about each person's well-being and success, and this was demonstrated through their actions every day. They went beyond customary expectations of a teacher, treating us in meaningful ways: a tea for the tea enthusiasts, French resources for the FSL teachers, and endless prizes of teacher supplies. Following the Tribes trail (a map outlining the natural progression of socialization that occurs among group members and the teacher-facilitator), Gail gradually released her leadership, but nurtured the classroom as needed, watching keenly as we flourished in front of her. Gail shared her life with us, encouraging us to open up to each other. Certainly, our additional Tribes certification days (outside of regular college hours) later in the fall brought the class even closer as we shared personal details in our large community circle and in small groups. It was here, particularly in the whole-class circle, that we felt each other's happiness and each other's pains. I'm not usually one for dramatics but I found myself in ridiculous and humorous situations I would have never have imagined myself in. I was in a safe environment with lots of support. Our groupings were different almost every time; that's not to say they were always random. Sometimes I found myself with people with similar interests, other times each of us seemed to have a close friend in the group of four. Sometimes, we were matched by pizza toppings, other times by the animal calls we used. Depending on the task and the goal it was evident that Gail's groupings had a purpose. It seemed we were grouped to feel safe and comfortable, but also to meet and understand the diversity in our classmates.

The snapshots that Gail regularly took reminded us of our time spent together and also allowed her to reflect on the friendships that were forming in the class. While some of the other cohorts were still unfamiliar with their classmates' names, our cohort could count on a familiar and friendly face throughout our days at the college. It was further evident by Christmas time, when our cohort had organized a personal gathering outside of the class that we were part of a strong learning community that extended beyond the walls of our classroom.

As the spring approached, we began interview preparation for our hopeful next step into school boards. In small groups we were matched with potential principals in mock interview format, a situation that can cause a lot of anxiety. Instead, we were able to gain more from the experience as our peers could provide positive constructive feedback having spent time practicing listening and effective communication skills. The personal friendships allowed for these interviews and academic work at large to feel less stressful since there were always people around to help or to listen. By the last day of the Tribes certification, nearing the end of our preservice year together, the feeling of love and compassion in the group was palpable.

In less than eight months, we had all grown individually and as a group. We each made a sharing/talking stick (a sacred object used by First Nations peoples to facilitate a talking circle), to use in our own future community circles. As referenced in Gail's reflection in *Whole Child Education* (Miller, 2010, p. 57), it is a powerful moment as people quietly and meaningfully create their stick, share a memory, and place their stick on a black cloth creating a star of positive energy. The true measure of the experience became evident to me when I took community circle practice into my final practicum of student teaching.

I had facilitated several community circles with my Grade 6 class, as a student teacher, using various objects to pass around, always silently and eagerly awaiting the last circle when I would reveal the talking stick I had made. I gave a brief introduction to my class about how I had learned community circle and my experience creating my sharing object in my cohort.

The students cautiously and gently passed the stick around the circle as each of them shared how they felt that day. The journal entries afterwards from these 11 and 12-year-olds further validated the process. They shared that they had learned so much about their classmates and how interesting they found their peers. They felt comforted that they weren't alone in their thoughts. It was evident they had a desire to learn about each other that had rarely been addressed in their education. My last day with the Grade 6 class was a tearful one. I played a slideshow of the times we had shared. I never would have imagined the gift that I received. The class presented me with a beautiful stick that one of the students had whittled, signed by everyone in the class. I was amazed that they had truly felt the importance of the talking stick, and I could see in their faces how happy they were to give me such a meaningful gift.

TRANSFORMATIVE LEARNING

While I learned a great deal about teaching holistically from Gail's leadership, I learned more about what it feels like to be taught holistically. I felt empowered, loved and cared for, and supported. Instead of learning *what* holistic teaching looks like, I learned *how* holistic teaching feels. I learned what it means to authentically connect and care unconditionally for a class of students, or rather a group of people. I felt I reached deeper reflections, learned about myself and learned about others, which all contributed to my success in a cooperative and collaborative community. I looked forward to Gail's class because I knew I would leave feeling energized and positive. I finally understood how intimate learning is. It's difficult to share ideas, explore one's curiosity and open up, characteristics associated with deep inner change and learning, without a sense of support and trust in one's classmates. We shared intimate details about our families and lives, strengthening our academic success. When a class works together to succeed as a whole and connect as human beings, then the academic content can be intertwined within the transformative experience. Tribes provides authentic opportunities for students to feel united in our increasingly disconnected world. This harmonization among students, people, and cultures is vital for us to learn and practice if we want to have a sustainable future.

Considering the significant amount of time children spend in school, it is essential that pedagogy remain pertinent and critically debated. Undoubtedly, our traditionally structured education system needs transformation, moving away from an overly competitive, if not oppressive, environment toward a system that reflects the organic, dynamic interconnectedness of the universe. Teaching holistically nurtures students wholly, validating their emotions. Tribes is one tool that provides a thoughtful framework which educators can use to help bridge the gap between academics and the heart.

REFERENCES

Gibbs, J. (2006). *Reaching all by creating tribes learning communities.* Windsor, CA: CenterSource Systems.

Macy, J., & Johnstone, C. (2012). *Active hope: How to face the mess we're in without going crazy.* Novato, CA: New World Library.

Miller, J. P. (2010). *Whole child education.* Toronto, ON: University of Toronto Press.

Schlitz, M. M., Vieten, C., & Amorok, T. (2007). *Living deeply: The art & science of transformation in everyday life.* (1 ed.). Oakland, CA: New Harbinger Publications.

CHAPTER 5

COLEGIO SAN FRANCISCO DE ASIS PARA NIÑOS SORDOS

A Chilean School for the Deaf

Ximena Barria Fernandez
University of Toronto

I have been a teacher for over 15 years and have worked at the same school for the deaf for most of those years, a school that was founded by a group of colleagues and me. Writing about my journey as an educator is not separate from the history of this school, and that is what I will present in this discussion: my evolving passion for teaching, the genesis of our school for the deaf and my hopes for its future. Firstly, I will offer a narrative of my personal journey as a teacher. Then I will review the history of my school and how we have been working on incorporating holistic perspectives in our teaching practices. Finally, I will explain my plans, expectations and my vision to make the school more inclusive for our students.

Teaching From the Thinking Heart, pages 43–53
Copyright © 2014 by Information Age Publishing
All rights of reproduction in any form reserved.

MY HISTORY AS AN EDUCATOR

To commence, I would like to state that being a teacher defines who I am. My career as an educator lies at the very core of my personal development. Two significant memories show how, from a very early age and throughout my development as a teenager, that all I really wanted to be when I grew up was a teacher. I remember being seven or eight years old, playing school with my dolls. Sometimes I would even coerce my little brother to play the role of one of my students. Even though my grandmothers were both teachers, I do not recall either of them sharing stories of their teaching experiences. As far as I can remember, we might have had some occasional conversations, just as I was finishing high school, but those conversations were never really encouraging. Neither grandmother wanted me to apply for teacher's college. They both provided seemingly good reasons for discouraging my career choice. They talked about how hard it was to teach, the low pay, and the fact that the true value and respect for the teaching profession, was simply scarce in Chile.

Despite my grandmothers' advice, I applied to eight teaching programs in three different universities. I got accepted in four of those programs, and finally decided to register in special education with a major in language and hearing disabilities. I chose special education, without having any prior experience working with people who have special needs, let alone did I know anything about deaf people. Yet, there I was, a 17 year old young woman, full of dreams about teaching and making a difference in the world.

My university years did nothing but strengthen the passion I had; every year I was more convinced that I had chosen the right path, and I felt deep inside that someday I would become not only a good teacher, but the teacher I had always dreamt of being. During this period I also began to immerse myself in the culture of people with disabilities, and particularly with deaf people. I still remember my lovely teacher of Chilean sign language, Mr. Juan Marin, who introduced himself to the class in very clear oral language, "Hello, my name is Juan Marin, I will be your teacher and I am deaf." I was shocked. I believed that deaf people were not capable of speaking and would often incorrectly refer to them as deaf-mute, as many people do. I learned also that some people are proud of their deafness. From that day on, my understanding of what it meant to be deaf changed with every new hearing impaired person I encountered.

Upon graduating I began to teach at a renowned and well-established school for the deaf. I was 23 years old and I was really terrified. In fact, during those first few years, teaching was very hard for me. I felt as if I did not possess the skill or knowledge that I needed to assist my students. I also often felt very helpless. What stopped me from quitting altogether was the connection that I was establishing with my students. Somehow their energy, their joy, and their trust worked like a fuel that fed my passion for teaching and learning and kept it constantly alive. That remarkable energy also inspired me to continue learning, to update my knowledge and to search for new tools that would help me to become the good teacher I always knew I would be.

In 1998, after working as a teacher at a very well recognized school for the deaf in Santiago, I was informed that the school could no longer keep its doors open. We learned of the imminent closure just two months before finishing the school year. Feeling shocked, yet knowing that there had been serious financial difficulties, we simply did not foresee that these difficulties were serious enough to lead to the ending of a school that had been working with deaf students for over 75 years.

We faced this unexpected and rather devastating situation with the fear that one feels when confronted with a seemingly insurmountable obstacle. There are not many schools for the deaf in Santiago, and back then educational programs that included deaf students in regular schools were rare. My colleagues and I were facing the very real possibility of not being able to work as teachers of the deaf. There was also the sobering fact that all those families were suddenly faced with how they were to continue educating their children. Space in the other three schools for the deaf in Santiago was limited; therefore, these students would have to go into mainstream schools, most of which were not prepared to support the needs of deaf students.

Together we outlined and carefully weighed the alternatives, assessing them in relation to our personal goals. We knew that we wanted to work with deaf students and were very committed to helping students from underprivileged backgrounds. We as teachers felt it was important to work at a place that could offer flexibility with respect to developing appropriate curriculum ideas and a suitable educational vision. Finally, we made a decision that took considerable courage. We agreed to create our own semi-private school for the deaf, administrated by us, and funded by the government.

THE SCHOOL'S BEGINNING:
SAN FRANCISCO DE ASSIS PARA NIÑOS SORDOS

It was December of 1998 and after many meetings, as I mentioned above, our group of eleven women decided to create a new educative option for families needing a school for deaf and hearing impaired students. Without having all the resources and completely naïve about what it would mean to create a school from the ground up, we worked hard together to obtain the funds to open *San Francisco de Asís para Niños Sordos*. Starting the school was indeed a turning point in my career and in my life. Without conscious planning, I was living another dream that I held in my heart, while studying to be a teacher in university. Although I thought the dream of having my own school would become a reality by the end of my career, there I was with twenty 6-year-olds, far before I ever thought owning a school would be possible.

Our school is located in a small, old, rented house which is located in an inner city neighborhood in Santiago. However, because there are not many schools for the deaf, we receive students from all areas of the city and even some from outside the city limits. The one-storey building has six small classrooms, a few offices and a patio with a big tree in the middle. Our landlord is the Roman Catholic church. Located directly beside us, the church lends us its large patio so that we can use the extra space during recess and for physical education classes. During winter time we use its big lounge, which is also a place where we conduct ceremonies or special activities.

Our school includes early childhood education, which means we accept babies as young as six-months old and preschool children. Our classes serve elementary students until they reach Grade 6. Like many schools for the deaf in Chile, we work with hard-of-hearing and deaf students in small groups of five to eight. The main mode of communication is oral language, but we do not forbid, nor deny the use of Chilean sign language. Our decision to communicate in this way is based on the principles of Total Communication, with a special emphasis on oral language.[1] We constantly switch between exclusively using oral language and the use of simultaneous communication (oral language accompanied by signs).

With the help and support of our own families, friends, and the families of the students, our school opened its doors in March, 1999, and our community began a wonderful journey. That first year was a mixture of emotions. Many of the important foundational elements of starting a school remained in flux. We actually began the year without having a legal resolution from the Ministry of Education. That process would last months; during those months we were not receiving any salary and we could not afford the many basic needs a school requires on a day-to-day basis. The parents' association bought the school desks. Furniture was even being brought from our own homes. Some of our relatives gave us second hand bookshelves. We actually worked on painting the classrooms and polishing the wood floors to have the place ready for the beginning of the school year.

At this time, our labors were extensive. For example, we attended meetings at the Board of Education, taught our lessons daily to the students, and even cleaned the washrooms. Despite all of these extra duties and challenges, we began to build a very special bond amongst ourselves and with the families of our students. Some of the family members knew about our economic situation and committed to taking care of us by bringing the school community all sorts of gifts, mostly food, even though the majority of our students came from low income homes. I always remember that first year as a big roller coaster, which at the end leaves you tired, yet with a very good and satisfying sensation.

In terms of our pedagogical project, the first aim we had as educators was to create a school that would provide deaf students with a quality education, the kind of education that would allow them a successful life in society. During those first years, we strongly focused on the development of academic outcomes, especially oral language development, math, and literacy skills. We were determined to prove that deaf students have many capacities and can be an important addition to Chilean society. To do that we worked hard on updating our knowledge as educators. We focused on learning new teaching strategies that would allow the achievement of all the learning outcomes we aimed to obtain. Up to a certain point, we did succeed. For example our students graduated to mainstream schools and did well academically. Some of the first generation students are now working, or enrolled in college or university. Almost all of them graduated from high school. Therefore, we knew that what we were doing in the classroom was effective for our students and believed that we were walking on the right pedagogical path.

FROM TRANSMISSION TO TRANSFORMATION

However, during the difficult journey of opening and trying to sustain the school, we began to have this feeling that something was missing, that the transmission approach to education, and specifically being constantly concerned about learning outcomes, was not fulfilling our teaching expectations. We felt as if we were perpetuating the practice of teaching students with special needs exclusively through drill and rote learning. This approach carries the implicit belief that people with disabilities are limited. Instead, the teachers at our school believe that a person with a disability is a person with different abilities; this person possesses an endless potential for learning. Thus, we began to search for something even though we were not so clear as to what it was exactly, but we knew it would give us some answers to our inquiries on how to improve the curriculum and pedagogical practices in our school.

That search first led us towards a Chilean biologist and philosopher called Humberto Maturana (2001) and his theory of the *Biology of Love.* Among his many postulates, we explored the idea that every human being is biologically a loving being, and our interactions are based on language and emotions that respect the other as a legitimate other. Language contributes to what it means to be human. In other words, the recursive interactions in language and emotions are what make us human beings (Maturana, 2001). The fact that every conversation is a flow of language and emotions was a foundational idea for us. Thus, we began to discuss how we could become more aware of our own emotions and the language that we use in our inter-actions with each other and our students.

During that time, some of us were working on our own personal development, exploring a variety of different modalities, ranging from psychotherapy to meditation. These pursuits we hoped would connect us to our emotional and spiritual selves. In a very informal and colloquial manner, we sat together and shared our experiences. Then we decided that we should work and help each other to walk the path to a deeper awareness of our feelings, emotions, and spirituality but always in a very respectful space, in which converges a diversity of personal backgrounds and life experiences. Fortunately, despite our differences, there was a total agreement on this new journey that we were anxious and excited to begin.

While developing an embodied understanding of Maturana's concepts and the importance of understanding how our emotions play out within ourselves and in our relationships, we explored the thoughts of Claudio Naranjo (2007) on personality and human dynamics. Naranjo is a Chilean psychiatrist known for his work in the integration of psychotherapy and spiritual traditions. He developed a model of human personality called *Enneagram of Personality* and created a program of personal and professional development called *Seekers After Truth* (SAT Program).

Naranjo (2007) writes that the apathy and discouragement of students towards school is the direct result of an educational system that is not providing opportunities for human development. Instead, school has become merely a system for transferring information. Naranjo refers to his philosophy of education as *Pedagogy of Love*. The philosophy espouses the notion that humans are all loving beings, but throughout life, through our woundedness and inner conflicts, we lose the capacity to love. Naranjo offers hope by explaining the importance of healing the emotions, thereby recovering a natural capacity to love and be loved.

Based on the proposals of Maturana and Naranjo and the interesting discussions that we were having at our monthly meetings, it became clear that in order to improve our students' achievements, we had to begin with a change or transformation within ourselves. Personal development and awareness of our own emotions were the keys to improving interactions in the classroom and thereby enhancing the quality of teaching and learning that we wished to offer our students. Embracing and examining our inner life would eventually shed light on our hidden personal wounds. This kind of deep reflection can ultimately lead to happiness and fulfilment but can also shed light on inner discomfort and emotional pain. I strongly believe that every educator needs to embrace this journey, whether difficult or not. Educators hold an awesome responsibility for their students, and if we truly believe that the purpose of education is to guide our pupils through their development—meaning body, mind, emotions, and spirituality—as teachers, we need to embrace and take conscious ownership for our own wholeness. The wholeness of our students can then be fostered authentically.

When a teacher has worked on his/her spiritual development and is aware of his/her emotions, it is easier to build a heartfelt connection with the students. Students, especially our young ones, can easily sense when a teacher is being honest. They are accustomed to reading facial expressions and body language and can even easily intuit, or pick up on, a teacher's mood. When the teacher honestly communicates their thoughts and desires, the students are more open towards the learning process.

With these propositions in mind and with the guidance of our school psychologist, we incorporated into our monthly teachers' meetings, activities that holistic educators typically practice, for example, guided imagery, body awareness, personal narratives, and discussions about fears, challenges, and accomplishments (Miller, 2000). The process has been extremely powerful. Although our process might seem simple, the main challenge underlying this work is the fact that we are opening a space to share and embrace emotions. Being intimate in this way is something that is not at all common in our society. Our culture tends to be very conservative with respect to sharing feelings in public. Emotions are only shared in the privacy of one's own home or maybe with a close friend.

NURTURING OUR SCHOOL COMMUNITY

Once we began to create awareness of our emotions in our role as educators, it was natural to confidently introduce different types of mindfulness activities with our students, such as relaxation, group massages, meditation, breathing, and body awareness. Through witnessing both teachers' and students' experiences, I notice how much our whole school community has been profoundly influenced. We are creating a strong sense of connectedness, through developing more trustful and honest relationships within our learning community. These embodied values are even extending to the families. A clear example of the school's connectedness was the creation of a community mandala.

A couple of years ago, we were celebrating our school anniversary, and one of the main activities we decided to do together was to create our mandala.[2] The process involved everyone from students, teachers, administrative staff, and families. Each group created a small mandala based on the question: what does the school mean to you? Then each mandala became a part of one large school mandala. Once we finished this creation, the school mandala was presented to the community at our anniversary ceremony. I will always remember the moment that I first saw this mandala. In that moment it became so clear to me that our school community is on the path of making a change towards a new approach to education. By introducing transpersonal psychology's practices, namely the sharing of our inner lives, we opened the doors to a transformational approach to learning. We not only share this psychological context with holistic education, we also share holistic education's aim to nurture the mind, the body, and the soul.

OUR FUTURE: A HISTORY ABOUT TO BE WRITTEN

The changes we have made in our school have opened new developmental opportunities for myself as an educator and for my students. However, the original purpose of the school project (which was to offer a high standard of education for deaf students) has not changed significantly. I still want to offer an effective education that ensures opportunities for the further academic and social learning of our deaf students. We have indeed made good advances with respect to establishing strong academic skills and providing opportunities for students to develop their inner lives. However, we are struggling with finding the learning opportunities that foster the social development of our students. This is a school for the deaf and the issue of isolation from the real world always underlies our concern for the students' futures. The students lack interactive experiences with their hearing peers.

I strongly believe that deaf and hearing impaired students do need a personalized education that connects to who they are becoming as individuals. I also agree with Vygotsky and his sociohistorical theory, which proposes that cultural and social interactions are important for human development and knowledge construction (Newman & Newman, 2007). If deaf students are in a school that is devoted exclusively for the deaf, they can receive a personalized and student-centred education in a small classroom. This intimacy allows teachers to develop most of the students' necessary skills, but unfortunately, these students will not be exposed to important interactions with their hearing peers. It is true that if deaf students go to mainstream schools, they will certainly develop better skills in terms of their social relationships. But when mainstream classrooms have over forty students, it is very difficult for teachers to offer the guidance and individual attention that a deaf student needs. Unfortunately, current public education in Chile is not offering the best setting for truly inclusive schooling.

As I have already indicated above, the impact that the transformational practices have had on our ability to fully embrace wholeness is evidenced on so many levels within our school community. There are significant changes in the educators, in our students, and even in the families. Therefore, it seems a natural progression to offer these holistic learning experiences to students who attend other schools. One way to offer hearing students this type of learning would be to change our school from a school for the deaf to an inclusive school, where hearing, hard of hearing, and deaf children learn together.

This school should have a flexible curriculum that would be respectful of the broad differences among students. There are some deaf students whose abilities would allow them to be incorporated into mainstream classes as soon as preschool or maybe at the first or second grade. There may be other deaf students who present different challenges, aside from deafness, such as intellectual disabilities. These students may not necessarily benefit from a full mainstream program. Hence for those students, the curriculum should allow them to receive part of their instruction in a separate classroom. However, these students still deserve plenty of opportunities, formal and informal, for social interaction with hearing peers.

The main challenge in making this project come true is to build a strong community which supports the ideals of holistic education. From my experience, this will require strengthening values such as respect and trust, learning to work collaboratively, and offering opportunities for self development (for educators and administrators). It is also important for educators to learn to listen to parents and students' perspectives, which is something we do not often do. Listening to their perspectives becomes a must if we want to achieve an integral development of our students.

The issue of curriculum and programs of study appears to be one of the biggest difficulties in this project. In order to receive government funding, we need to ensure that our curriculum follows government standards. Currently, the programs of study, outlined by the Ministry of Education, are developed with a mandatory structure, which is very subject-based and does not allow for very much flexibility. Our teaching staff believes that we must continue to develop more curriculum strategies that encourage connections between subjects and more mindfulness activities in the classroom.

Additionally, if we are to incorporate mindfulness activities in the classroom, it must be done in a systematic and purposed manner, within the government's more rigid standards. We have been incorporating mindfulness activities into our classes and are continuing to make these practices an essential feature of our teaching approach. Although it may sound difficult to merge standardized curriculum with a more flexible educational perspective, I believe that with a community that is strong and well connected with each other, this integration is entirely possible. Although my future educational project calls for a meaningful shift from a school that is exclusively for the deaf to an elementary school for deaf and nondeaf students, the current mission and vision of our school should not change dramatically (see appendix). The school will still espouse a transformational approach, which encompasses the whole person, and nurtures the mind, body, emotions, and soul of each member of the learning community.

NOTES

1. Total Communication is a philosophical approach to teaching deaf students which incorporates all means of modalities to communicate, such as speech, signs, finger spelling, natural gestures, lip reading, and body language (Mayer, 2012).
2. Mandala in Sankrit means healing circle. It is an art form that uses a circular format, representing a cosmic connection and wholeness. Many different cultures and religions use mandalas for meditation. Carl Jung incorporated them in psychological therapies (Schrade, Tronsky, & Kaiser, 2011).

APPENDIX

Mission Statement: The School for the Deaf San Francisco de Asís

San Francisco de Asís School for the Deaf offers an educative option that is focused on a transpersonal approach to enhancing the life of the deaf person: body, emotions, intellect, and spirit. The school offers a dynamic perspective which allows for discovery and the highest potential for deaf children and youth. The school facilitates a student's capacity to: (a) adapt to a constantly changing world, (b) seek their own development as free human beings, (c) be in harmony with themselves and their environment, and (d) become agents of a more humane and fair world.

Vision of the School for the Deaf San Francisco de Asís

Our dream . . . is to nurture a conscious and interactive space in which all members develop and connect in an atmosphere of respect, participation, trust, and freedom. Our core pedagogical concern includes a respect for all the essential elements of what it means to be human. We seek to offer deaf students an education which allows them to live life fully through innovative and active curricular methods that are directly related to children's interests and meaningful learning. We believe this generates in our students' openness to experience, the experience of awe, the freedom of expression, interest in self-knowledge, and knowledge of the world. Finally, our school inspires a capacity to face new challenges with creativity; the enjoyment of emotion, love, and belonging; and the ability to dream a future into reality.

Note: Both of the above have been translated from the original document created in 2009 by the staff of the school for the deaf San Francisco de Asís.

REFERENCES

Colegio San Francisco de Asís para niños sordos. (2009). *Proyecto educativo del colegio San Francisco de Asís para niños sordos.* Santiago, Chile.

Maturana, H. (2001). *Emociones y lenguaje en educación y política (10ma ed.).* Santiago, Chile: Editorial Dolmen.

Mayer, C. (2012). A role for total communication in 2012. *BATOD Association Magazine,* 8–9.

Naranjo, C. (2007). *Cambiar la educación para Cambiar el Mundo (1a ed.).* Santiago, Chile: Editorial Cuarto Propio.

Miller, J. P. (2000). *Education and the soul: Towards a spiritual curriculum.* Albany: State University of New York.

Newman, B., & Newman, P. (2007). *Theories of human development.* Mahwah, N.J.: Lawrence Erlbaum Associates.

Schrade, C., Tronsky, L., & Kaiser, D. H. (2011). Physiological effects of mandala making in adults with intellectual disability. *The Arts in Psychotherapy,* (38), 109–113.

CHAPTER 6

EXPLORING PLAY AND MINDFULNESS IN EARLY CHILDHOOD

Melanie Viglas
University of Toronto

The education system's purpose is to prepare our children for the responsibility of inheriting important social roles in the future (Elias, 2006). In our dog-eat-dog world, where advances in technology are pulling us further away from each other, increasing our feelings of isolation and separateness, it is no wonder that our education system is struggling. It seems that as a society we are losing touch with the connection we have to each other, if not the entire natural world, and we are suffering the consequences. I've discovered that teaching mindfulness in early childhood has the potential to cultivate young children's understanding of our shared humanity while providing a wealth of benefits to help children achieve success in school.

My teaching career path began with a love for children. Throughout my master's program, I was instilled with the idea that a child-centered pedagogy was the "best" approach. Whenever I came across a teacher whose teaching style did not fit this pedagogy, I was judgmental and critical of them and their practice.

Teaching From the Thinking Heart, pages 55–60
Copyright © 2014 by Information Age Publishing

My first practicum placement was in a public school of mostly immigrant children. My associate teacher was another graduate of the same program as me so I was excited to observe a child-centered classroom. The moment I stepped into the classroom, my host teacher "apologized" for the different things I was about to see that didn't conform to the child-centered philosophy: desks in rows, assigned seating, mostly teacher-led activities, textbooks, even worksheets. The teacher explained that child-centered pedagogy doesn't always work, but I could sense that there was guilt in this statement, perhaps because she felt that she had failed to implement something that she believed in.

After spending my four-week block with the students in this classroom and observing the program that my host teacher was providing, I was able to reflect on the efforts she had made to accommodate the needs of these children. She had set up the daily routine so the children always knew what to do and how long they had to do it. Children interacted with their work and with her. Although this "teacher-centered" program seemed to run smoothly and children *were* learning, I recognized something important was lost. While the various components of the program seemed successful at meeting the academic needs of the students, the sense of community was missing. Also, the curious and exploratory nature of children struck me as tamped down. The structure of the program intended to focus on acquiring the academic skills needed for these English Language Learners to catch up and perform at grade-level meant there was no time for children to interact with each other and no time for children do what children do best—play.

THE IMPORTANCE OF PLAY

My next practicum placement was in an independent school where most children came from upper-middle class families. The school's philosophy reflected holistic pedagogy, and I finally got a taste of what it means to teach the whole child. During this placement, I learned about the importance of a warm, supportive play environment. Through holistic play-based learning experiences, children learn how to be mindful of others' intentions, emotions, and beliefs. In turn, children learn the skills they need in order to problem-solve, reflect, and accept points of view that differ from their own. These skills are crucial to acquiring the learning strategies and tools required for approaching new experiences with interest, curiosity, and confidence (Pascal, 2009).

Following this engaging practicum, I got my first teaching job in a public school in one of the more marginalized communities of Toronto. I taught Senior Kindergarten to 27 children in the morning and 27 children in the afternoon. Both groups were culturally diverse and a high percentage of my students came from backgrounds with low socioeconomic status.

The administration (and some of the parents) expected me to teach academic skills rather than allow children time to play. In fact, one of the most significant factors affecting young children's school experience today is the pressure for early learning (Petrash, 2002). In her book *Endangered Minds: Why Children Don't Think*, Jane Healy (1990) explains the price we pay for this stressful, accelerated academic instruction:

> Before brain regions are myelinated (and nerves have the outer coating needed to transmit impulses), they do not operate efficiently. For this reason, trying to make children master academic skills for which they do not have the requisite maturation may result in mixed-up patterns of learning. I would contend that much of today's academic failure results from academic expectations for which students' brains were not prepared but which were bulldozed into them anyway. (p. 67)

It was true that the majority of my students came to my classroom with few academic skills, but what concerned me was their lack of social and emotional skills. These children had not had many opportunities to develop self-regulation and social-emotional skills and what they needed was to play. How was I to teach these young children to read and write when they didn't even know how to regulate their emotions? As stated in the Every Child, Every Opportunity document: "Self-regulation is the cornerstone of development and is the central building block of early learning . . . [it] is the ability to adapt one's emotions, behaviors, and attention to the demands of the situation." (p. 4). Play environments provide young children with optimal learning conditions to practice self-regulation. These experiences will allow them to learn how to get along with each other, resolve conflicts in constructive ways, and develop the necessary skills in negotiating social situations (Bodrova & Leong, 2008; Shonkoff & Phillips, 2000; Diamond et al., 2007). My attempts to incorporate play in the curriculum was met with, "Remember, Melanie, they've already played in JK."

DISCOVERING MINDFULNESS

I became increasingly frustrated and anxious over the year with the constant tension I experienced between what I felt I should be doing and what I actually could do. I knew that I had to re-evaluate my beliefs and my values to adapt to my situation as suggested by Palmer (2007):

> The most practical thing we can achieve in any kind of work is insight into what is happening inside of us as we do it. The more familiar we are with our inner terrain, the more surefooted our teaching—and living—becomes. (p. 6)

In my second year of teaching, I discovered the teachings of Eckhart Tolle in *The Power of Now*. I began to practice yoga and even attended a 10-day silent meditation course. My newfound understandings and passion for yoga and meditation made me eager to experiment with implementing learning into my kindergarten class, so I began reading books about mindfulness and holistic education.

Since young children already possess a "beginner's mind" and are able to live in the moment, it felt fitting to introduce mindfulness practices to my students as a potential strategy to enhance their self-regulation and social-emotional skills. Teaching mindfulness practices in early childhood is as simple as introducing children to the transformative power of their breathing. By guiding children through simple breath awareness exercises, they can become aware of their emotions (Kaiser-Greenland, 2010). When children practice being mindful of their breathing and emotions, they tap into the connection between their bodies and their minds. They can learn to use this awareness to regulate their emotions and behaviors when they need to (Jennings & Greenberg, 2009). My students spent the majority of their time using these developing skills during their in-class play. Further, they could better negotiate their learning through these experiences. They loved practicing mindfulness, and I was amazed at how it created a sense of community in the classroom.

I continued to implement mindfulness and developed a program incorporating these exercises in kindergarten. Although I knew the benefits of the program, I still struggled with the rest of the school. My holistic curriculum alienated the administration and most of my colleagues, who felt "best practice" was proven by test scores. This ongoing conflict led me to take a leave of absence from teaching to pursue doctoral studies.

MINDFULNESS IN EARLY CHILDHOOD

Research on teaching mindfulness to children is very much in its infancy, but the evidence is promising. I have gone back to school in order to contribute to the field of mindfulness in early childhood education. As regulatory systems are organized early in life, it is important to attend to the development of these skills while these core brain functions tend to be more plastic. Nurturing the development of these skills during these sensitive periods of brain development is crucial to young children's competence in all areas (Bodrova & Leong, 2008; Mustard, 1999).

Joseph Pearce, (1993) a well-known author on child development and creativity, describes young children's ability to be mindful in the following account of the importance of play:

> Play is the royal road to childhood happiness and adult brilliance . . . Children at play are not doing one thing with their hands or bodies, thinking something else in their minds, and speaking something else with their voice as we adults tend to do. They are totally absorbed in their play-world, absolutely one with their talk of play . . . Through this discipline, true concentration, and one-pointedness develop. (p. 41)

Young children enter the educational system at a time when many developmental changes are occurring. This period is marked by a natural sense of curiosity and exploration that makes them primed to learn through play. Play-based early childhood programs are designed to reflect the developmental qualities of young children, and research has indicated that the quality of developmentally appropriate programs predicts improved child outcomes in early childhood settings (Pianta, 2003).

Through educational programs that support children's social and emotional development, we can find ways to teach children how to connect to themselves, to others, and to the world around them. Teaching children mindfulness is one way that imparts not only a sense of our shared humanity but also the understanding that everything is interconnected. Once I discovered the benefits of practicing mindfulness in my own life, I was amazed at how much of a positive impact it had on my relationships with my students and how it helped me plan a program that I believed in. A curriculum that provides children with opportunities to practice mindfulness has the potential to support and improve their wellbeing, building an important foundation for them to reach their potential in school. Zins and Elias (2009) suggest:

> . . . genuinely effective schools-those that prepare students not only to pass tests at school but also to pass the test of life-are finding that social-emotional competence and academic achievement are interwoven and that integrated, coordinated instruction in both areas maximizes students' potential to succeed in school and throughout their lives. (p. 233)

All children need to play and all children will benefit from being taught holistically. I've witnessed how mindfulness transcends diversity with its profound effect on all children. It makes sense to turn to a practice that is so simple yet so powerful. Given the flexibility of young children's brains, introducing mindfulness in early childhood programs has the potential to provide our children with the life skills they will need in order to make a positive impact on our society.

REFERENCES

Bodrova, E., & Leong, D. J. (2008). Developing self-regulation in kindergarten. *Beyond the journal: Young children on the Web.* National Association for the Education of Young Children.

Diamond, A., Barnett, W. S., Thomas, J., & Munro, S., (2007). Preschool program improves cognitive control. *Science. 318,* 1387–1388.

Elias, M., J. (2006). The connection between academic and social-emotional learning. In M. J. Elias & H. Arnold (Eds.), *The educator's guide to emotional intelligence and academic achievement* (pp. 4–14). Thousand Oaks, CA: Corwin Press.

Healy, J. (1990). *Endangered minds: Why children don't think.* NY: Touchstone.

Jennings, P., & Greenberg, M. (2009). *The prosocial classroom: Teacher social and emotional competence in relation to student and classroom outcomes.* Review of Educational Research. *79*(1), 491–525.

Kaiser Greenland, S. (2010). *The mindful child.* New York, NY: Simon and Schuster.

Palmer, P. J. (2007). *The courage to teach: Exploring the inner landscape of a teacher's life.* San Francisco: Jossey-Bass.

Pianta, R. C. (2003). *Experiences in p-3 classrooms: The implications of observational research for redesigning early education.* New York, NY: Foundation for Child Development.

Shonkoff, J., & Phillips, D. (2000). *From neurons to neighborhoods.* Washington, DC: National Academy Press.

Zins, J. E., & Elias, M. J. (2007). Social and emotional learning: Promoting the development of all students. *Journal of Educational and Psychological Consultation, 17*(2–3), 233–255.

CHAPTER 7

ME, MYSELF, AND I

The Paradox of the Authentic Self

Michèle Irwin
University of Toronto

> *I celebrate myself, and sing myself,*
> *And what I assume you shall assume,*
> *For every atom belonging to me as good belongs to you.*
>
> —Walt Whitman, *Song of Myself*

What am I when I stand at the classroom door? Before I turn the knob and go in, what do I bring with me? I don't walk through the door merely as *teacher*. This would be to reduce myself, a whole woman, to a word that signifies merely a single role. It hardly captures all of me. Before and after the classroom, I regard myself as mother, writer, and teacher. There's more: daughter, sister, aunt, friend, student, reader, lover, child, dreamer, dancer, and hiker. I am even what my daydreams suggest, world traveler, artist, cellist, comedian, and sphinx. I have to admit, like Whitman (1892), "I am large. I am multitudes." The authentic self contains many selves. What then of this myriad self distilled to the moment before I step into a room and teach?

It is easiest for me to see myself most simply as threefold. I am a mother, writer, and teacher. The words *I am. I Am.* I am a whole woman made up

Teaching From the Thinking Heart, pages 61–65
Copyright © 2014 by Information Age Publishing

of three identities; three parts to the whole, a woman with fears, thoughts, beliefs and the strength to carry out a life. This is who *I Am*. Why does this matter? There is a knot that needs tying. Two threads must be tied together where selfhood meets authenticity.

Authenticity may be selfhood expressed truthfully outside of myself. To know my soul, then, is to understand the root and expression of my authenticity. I must surrender to the task of self-exploration. The deconstruction of the selves that make up me is unsettling, but it is good. If I find the courage to do this work, liberating what all makes me, including my creativity, light and even despair, and to teach from this knowledge, then I also render invisible to anyone outside of me these selves within the self. Paradox.

I teach a curriculum. I also teach womanhood. I teach how to be a public servant and citizen. I matter. But I matter only insomuch as I serve others. As mother, writer, and teacher, I give. I give of myself. I give enough and not enough at the same time. I matter in the extreme, and I matter not at all.

Emerson (1926) offers, "Persons are supplementary to the primary teaching of the soul" (p. 195). Multiple paradoxes exist in Emerson's 'simple statement,' especially if we extend it to a classroom context: the paradox of the invisibility of the multiple selves that house the soul that is the teacher; the paradox that her own soul is the student's true teacher; and the paradox that the person is fundamental (at the same time as supplemental) to the primary teaching of the soul. This final paradox being the two threads in need of knotting, as soulful authenticity extends to meet action in the outside world.

Whitman (1892) writes in *Song of Myself*, "Writing and talk do not prove me/I carry the plenum of proof and every thing else in my face/With the hush of my lips I wholly confound the skeptic." It matters who I am, and how I present myself. My face and bearing reveal the condition of my soul. Emerson's paradox and Whitman's poetry suggest that even without action I am revealed. I am rarely without action, though, and so I am always in some way revealed.

My authentic self is in its finest form as Emerson (1926) posits, "When (soul) breathes through his intellect, it is genius; when it breathes through his will, it is virtue; when it flows through his affection, it is love" (p. 191). I suggest that this is when I am egoless, when my multiple selves are unified, when I have surrendered to my fearlessness as completely as I have to my despair, and when I feel unattached to my human form. This state, found in moments of passion, in nature, in laughter, in honest intellectual engagement, in creativity ought to be catalogued and described, the context of the moment understood, so when I stand at the classroom door I can summon it, return to it so my authentic self becomes cloak and habit.

The antithesis to authenticity, the hazard of in-authenticity, is revealed when "the blindness of the intellect begins when it would be something of itself. The weakness of the will begins when the individual would be something of himself" (Emerson, 1926, p. 191). The tension of the opposites has in these situations, lost its strength; the demands of the external world impinge on internal stasis. My body is felt. I feel pain or fatigue. Time pressures me. I become aware of myself, of my selves. I feel the demands of mother, the fears of writer, and the stresses of teacher. My unified authenticity is replaced by a splintering off the individual selves as they respond to the world independently. My students may see, "I am not the poet of goodness only, I do not decline to be the poet of wickedness also" (Whitman, 1892).

But who am I in synthesis?

I am Mother. To mother is to create. But in the moments of transition where the birth of my children marked the moment of letting go to let life, I began to prepare my own redundancy. Whitman (1892) writes, "I teach straying from me, yet who can stray from me? I follow you whoever you are from the present hour/My words itch at your ears till you understand them." As mother, I exist and I don't.

Piaget asserts that within their first year infants learn object permanence through touch. In other words, I continued to exist for my infant daughters even when I left the room. Piaget did not, however, describe the object *im*permanence learned in young adulthood. If I have been an authentic mother, present and true with the humility my role requires, I will love and be loved, but I will not, in the end, be necessary. From *Song of Myself*: I exist as I am, that is enough/If no other in the world be aware I sit content/And if each and all be aware I sit content" (Whitman, 1892). Mother stands at the classroom door, humbly preparing for her own redundancy.

As a writer, I look to literature for inspiration. Shakespeare, Emerson, Whitman, make sense of soul for me, and provide a gateway to authenticity. Literature is creation, and does not propose an absolute knowing, but allows the reader to find meaning at will. "There is in all great poets a wisdom of humanity which is superior to any talents they exercise" (Emerson, 1926, p. 204), suggesting Emerson's "breath of the soul" has spoken through the words of the writer. These writers, I imagine, have stepped away from the corporeal and the limits of talent to let the wisdom of the soul through. The ego feeds the writer only enough to motivate action and behavior, but then becomes quiet to hear the whispers of the soul.

These are forces that act in me when I write. The struggle between my brash and obstinate will and my patient soul has made me cry. Too often, my will and ego bully my soul, thinking that logic and talent prevail. However, "The soul looketh steadily forwards, creating a world always before her, leaving worlds always behind her. She has no dates, nor rites, nor persons, nor specialties, nor men. The soul knows only the soul; all else is idle weeds for her wearing" (Emerson, 1926, p. 198). The self that is ego and the self that is soul are in a contest that is no contest. And, so, my soul is patient and impatient. She understands the process of taming my will and focusing my ego, but she is impatient for my true expression. "The soul is superior to its knowledge, wiser than any of its works. The great poet makes us feel our own wealth, and then we think less of his compositions" (Emerson, 1926, p. 205). But the soul teases the ego into thinking the work will belong to the ego in the end, rather than to the world.

Writer stands before the classroom door, carrying with her the struggle between ego and soul.

I am Teacher. And I ready myself to go through the door with enough knowledge and never enough knowledge. I have planned my lesson, but it may not be the right lesson. Teaching requires the courage to not know. Whitman (1892), in *Song for Myself*: "A child said, What is the grass? Fetching it to me with full hands/How could I answer the child? I do not know what it is any more than he." As a teacher, I teach what I know. I learn what I can, and share it, but again, I inevitably encounter limits. Teaching, then, is facilitating. I teach content, but I also teach learning. I bring to the classroom youthful awe for the subject that I've chosen to master. This is my responsibility. In turn, I ask my students to accept responsibility for their learning,

> Stop this day and night with me and you shall possess the origin of all poems,
> You shall possess the good of the earth and sun, (there are millions of suns left,)
> You shall no longer take things at second or third hand, nor look through the
>   eyes of the dead, nor feed on the spectres in books,
> You shall not look through my eyes either, nor take things from me,
> You shall listen to all sides and filter them from your self. (Whitman, 1892)

I am just one source of knowledge. I am good enough for now. My authentic teacher is at the same time a student and a master. I define my teaching identity more by the beliefs I hold about good teaching than I do by the techniques of that good teaching. Teaching shares and allows worldly and soulful learning.

Here: *I am*. Mother, writer and teacher, doorknob in hand, ready to greet my students. My unified self has made peace with my redundancy; my ego-soul struggle; and I understand my students will move beyond me. My soul asks me to speak. It asks me to facilitate the freeing of other souls. This is the imperative of the paradox. I am larger when I am multiplied, but my soul achieves unification. I have amplified each of my multiple voices, but my soul demands distillation into one voice. My action proves authentic when it aligns with this voice.

> I bequeath myself to the dirt to grow from the grass I love,
> If you want me again look for me under your boot-soles. (Whitman, 1892)

This is the great moment for me, myself and I, mother, writer and teacher. The strange and uplifting moment when I am everything and nothing, in plain sight and invisible, when my words and actions are singular, when I am fragmented and whole, necessary and redundant. This is the great moment when I have given myself completely.

REFERENCES

Emerson, R. W. (1926). *Emerson's essays.* New York: Harper Colophon Books.
Whitman, W. (1892). Song of Myself. The Poetry Foundation. Retrieved from http:// poetryfoundation.org/poem/174745

CHAPTER 8

SOUL TO SOUL— TEACHER TO STUDENT

Julia Verhaeghe
University of Toronto

CLASSROOM COMMUNITY: DISMANTLING THE GUARD

Imagine walking into a room full of strangers and sharing your life story. What parts would you leave out? How would you transform your personal narrative as a defense against unknowable reactions? How would you transform yourself? At the beginning of a course, both teacher and students are confronted with just this: a room full of strangers. It is the teacher's responsibility to facilitate the creation of a space where strangers become whole people. I think it is unrealistic to assume that all students will become friends—they will not. A healthy classroom community is not necessarily a group of friends; it is a place where students feel comfortable in their bodies, free to express themselves while respecting others, and nourished as whole people. This raises a question: How can we, as teachers, facilitate the creation of a healthy classroom community?

I believe multiple layers of armor protect our souls. Palmer (1998) claims these virtual barriers "reduce our vulnerability" but cause us to "disconnect from students, from subjects, and even from ourselves" (p. 17). In a healthy classroom community, however, both teacher and students feel safe enough

Teaching From the Thinking Heart, pages 67–72
Copyright © 2014 by Information Age Publishing
All rights of reproduction in any form reserved.

to lower their shields and make themselves vulnerable. Only then are soul-to-soul connections possible.

During my first few years of teaching, I have learned a few community-building techniques. First of all, whether it is with small children or adults, I begin every lesson with a 5–10 minute "warmer." This is a term I learned from a British teacher trainer in Thailand. These warmers are meant to relax the students (and teacher) in preparation for the lesson. Some warmers are a little competitive, but my favorite are those that nourish whole-group bonds. For example, in the *Word Association Circle*, students sit in a circle and create a chain of associated words. One student (or the teacher) begins by saying any word. The next student in the circle must say the first word that comes to his or her mind upon hearing the preceding word. Then the third student must say a word that relates to the second word, and so on. The word chain may sound something like this: hot-sun-moon-night-bed-etc. It gets interesting, though, when a student says a word whose relation to the preceding word is not apparent. For example, one student says "bed," and the next student says "frog." In this case, the second student must explain why his or her mind made this connection. Perhaps the student has a stuffed animal frog that he or she sleeps with every night. I like this warmer because the individuality of each student is recognized as part of a larger whole.

I have received great feedback about warmers from a variety of students. A few years ago, I spent a month and a half in Tamil Nadu, India, volunteering as an ESL teacher at a school for children without homes. Besides teaching the grade three and four classes for an hour each day, I taught a conversational English class to the Indian school teachers in the evenings. During our first class together, the teachers sat in silence with straight backs and pens ready. When I asked them to stand up to play a warmer game, I could tell they were uncomfortable. However, after a few days, the games grew on them. One of the teachers gave me a written comment at the end of the course. She wrote, "In your class, I like it. The first time enter the class your game. I like this game." More recently, I received written feedback from an advanced-level group of international students. One student wrote, "I like the first activities of each morning in order to wake us up."

How do warmers build classroom community? Warmers counteract students' inhibitory tendencies, which are especially pronounced in adult classes. In his book *Principles of Language Learning and Teaching* (5th ed.), Douglas Brown (2007) defines inhibition as a defensive force "to protect a fragile ego, to ward off ideas, experiences, and feelings that threaten to dismantle the organization of values and beliefs on which appraisals of self-esteem have been founded" (p. 157). In other words, we inhibit ourselves to protect our self-esteem by eliminating the possibility of failure. Warmers break down inhibitions as spontaneity is encouraged and wrong answers are nonexistent. These simple games help create a classroom culture where students feel comfortable enough to unlearn their inhibitory tendencies and reveal their true selves to their supporting peers and to me.

Another community-building technique I have tried involves collaborative rule making. Every school where I have taught has required that time is set aside on the first day of class to review school policy and classroom rules. This procedure has the potential to be both dry and patronizing, especially with adult students. As a way to revamp this dreary policy proclamation, I usually ask my students to create their own classroom rule not mentioned on the official list. These are rules all members of the class should follow, including the teacher. If the students take the activity seriously (i.e., don't write, "Eat pizza every day"), I promise them I will follow their rules. I first tried this activity with a group of teenage, intermediate-level ESL students at a private language school. I collected the students' rules anonymously and compiled them into a document entitled "*Our* Classroom Rules." Here are a few rules these students wrote (in my words):

1. The teacher should spend individual time with each student.
2. Students should feel free to share their opinions, but always respect other classmates.
3. We should be able to eat in class. It's hard to learn when you're hungry.
4. No homework on Fridays. We need the weekend to relax.

I kept my promise. I never gave homework on Fridays, allowed the students to eat in class, and tried to spend time with each student every day. The students themselves were responsible for Rule #2, which I had to remind them of from time to time.

This type of collaboration between the teacher and students challenges what Paulo Freire (2009) calls *narrative education*, in which the "students are the depositories and the teacher is the depositor" of knowledge (p. 163). Freire differentiates between the narrative teacher and the humanist teacher. The humanist's "effort must be imbued with a profound trust in people and their creative power. To achieve this, they must be partners of the student in their relations with them" (p. 166). Whether it is writing classroom rules, choosing essay topics, or having a student teach a lesson, I have found that teacher-facilitated student input in the classroom establishes a community where students feel trusted, valued, and cared for. By encouraging students to take charge of their own learning, I trust the students to take the activity seriously, value their opinions, and as a result, care for them as individuals who are part of a greater whole. Like warmers, student input helps create a classroom community where students feel safe enough to let their guards down.

Moreover, a soul-to-soul connection between teacher and student requires that the teacher, too, be trusted, valued, and cared for by the students.

I have found that when I give students the freedom to trust, value, and care for me, they do. For example, when I taught an advanced grammar class of international teens, I asked each student to prepare a small presentation about a topic that interested them. These presentations were not graded (as they were not a part of the curriculum), but they counted toward their class participation mark. Students presented a variety of topics including how air conditioners work, traditional festivals in their home countries, and a visual art analysis. One student prepared a 20-minute presentation on Spanish history from the Middle Ages to present day. After the presentation, she told me she had chosen the topic for me because she had remembered my saying on the first day of class that I knew nothing about Spanish history. It was important to her that I know about the history of her country. When a teacher is cared for in this way by her students, she too can let her guard down, bear her soul, and build a deep-rooted bond with them.

A healthy classroom community where safety, trust, value, and care thrive establishes the conditions for building soul-to-soul connections; however, community alone is not enough. It is the teacher's responsibility to recognize that students are *whole* people, not just "brains on sticks."

RECOGNIZING THE WHOLE STUDENT

In order to connect with a student's soul, I first must recognize that the student has one in the first place, which can be difficult to do in a system that seems to value "intellect" above all other classroom virtues. Recently, I have been making a conscious effort to notice the wholeness of my students.

For about two years, I have been volunteering as a literacy tutor with a local community organization. For two hours every week, I meet with a woman who is determined to improve her literacy skills to get her GED. To respect her confidentiality, I will refer to this literacy learner as Sada. Over the past few years, Sada and I have developed a close bond, a soul-to-soul connection, but it was not always this way. During our second month together, Sada repeatedly did not show up for our scheduled tutoring session. The next time I saw her, I told her she should tell me beforehand if she had to cancel, and she has ever since. Even so, after being stood up, I put up a guard when interacting with Sada. This barrier protected me from being disappointed again. As I have gotten to know her, however, I have learned that Sada is a trauma survivor. She has endured incredible hardship that has impacted her holistically. Community-based researcher and educator Jenny Horsman (1999) suggests that since trauma impacts the whole person, education of trauma survivors must be equally holistic. Horsman believes a holistic approach to literacy education involves "considering each aspect of the person, becoming aware of the impact of trauma on all aspects of the person, and recognizing gains and shifts in sensitivity" (p. 169–170). After learning about Sada's past trauma, I began to see her as a whole person with a mind, body, and soul. By examining Sada's behavior holistically, I realized that perhaps she stood me up to protect herself by creating a distance between us. Wounded souls need protection. If you never get close to someone, there is no chance of being hurt. After making this realization and seeing Sada as a whole person, I gradually lowered my guard, and so did she. Now, we have established a strong connection built on mutual trust and understanding. I hope to continue learning together for many years to come.

In addition to recognizing how the past can influence the present whole person, I have also tried supplementing grammar-focused ESL curricula with creative activities to nourish the whole student. For example, I taught an advanced-level group of students who were required to learn the complex passive form (e.g., "It is said that..."). To make this grammar structure a little more interesting, I introduced the topic by asking the students to read creation myths from different cultures (e.g., "It is said that before time began there was only darkness."). Then I asked my teenaged students to write their own creation myths in pairs, being sure to use a few examples of the complex passive form. After writing, we all sat in a circle, and each pair read their story to the class. As the class listened, we closed our eyes and visualized the creation of the world as depicted by the tale. When the story was finished, we opened our eyes, and took two minutes to sketch one of our visualizations, which we then showed the class. As the teacher, I also participated in this activity which I think made the students (eight 16–17 year olds, and one 60 year old) feel more comfortable doing such a "nonacademic" exercise. The activity was a great success. It felt relaxing to close our eyes during the storytelling, and the students were all eager to see each other's drawings once the reading was over. The grammar was not the focus—imagination and creativity was. The students were given the chance to express themselves and let their souls sing. After this activity, I felt my soul-to-soul connection with each student had grown stronger.

When I think about a soul-to-soul bond, I tend to picture two overlapping circles: two wholes connecting. The circumference of a circle has an infinite number of sides, as does the boundary of a person. Recognizing the whole student does not imply that the student's whole being is knowable, but that its existence is acknowledged. Through this recognition of wholeness, meaningful connections can be made between a teacher's soul and her students'.

Soul-to-soul connection is almost impossible to describe in words. It can only be felt physically and spiritually. It is my intuition that recognizes a soul-to-soul connection with a student—the same intuition that told me to become a teacher instead of a biologist. Even though I may intuitively feel deeply connected with some students, I do not feel a strong bond with them all. I am not trying to fool myself; there are certain students with whom I have never been able to get beyond the superficial teacher-student relationship. I cannot force a connection. What I *can* do, though, is my best to facilitate the creation of conditions where students' souls are safe and acknowledged, through building a healthy classroom community and recognizing the whole student. Human connections are the heart of education. When souls collide, real learning is possible.

REFERENCES

Brown, D. (2007). *Principles of language learning and teaching* (5th ed.). White Plains, New York: Pearson Education Inc.

Freire, P. (2009). Race/ethnicity: Multidisciplinary global contexts. *Pedagogy of the Oppressed.* (Chapter 2). 2(2), 163–174.

Horsman, J. (1999). *Too scared to learn: Women, violence, and education.* (169–214). Toronto: McGilligan.

Palmer, P. J. (1998). *The courage to teacher.* San Francisco, CA: John Wiley & Sons, Inc.

CHAPTER 9

CULTIVATING CURIOSITY

Inquiry in an International Baccalaureate Classroom

Rebecca Ryder
University of Toronto

My childhood was filled with summer camps, drama workshops, and volunteer experiences. Although I loved my time in school and was very successful in a traditional classroom environment, I realized from a very early age, that many of my most significant learning moments happened outside of those four walls and through nonconventional teaching. The moments I remember most vividly, the ones I learned the most from, seemed to be when I was given the opportunity to explore my passions, discover more about my personal interests, and make emotional, as well as intellectual connections. My teacher's college application, written over ten years ago, states, "At times it is a teachers responsibility to teach, but more often it is a teacher's responsibility to offer a wide range of opportunities for children to explore, create, connect, and discover. I feel strongly about the value of experiences outside, as well as inside, the classroom, and I believe strongly in the value of educating the whole child."

Teaching From the Thinking Heart, pages 73–81

In a description of what it means to teach to the whole child, Miller (2010) includes Gandhi's perspectives on basic education, specifically his commitment to the harmonious development of the 'head, heart, and hands" of the student (p. 8). Miller also explains that the whole child is the body, mind, and spirit, an *indivisible whole*. I believe that the best way for these three aspects of the child to be reached is through cultivating curiosity. When motivated to find out more, curiosity and interest can grow into passion, and passion ignites all aspects of the self. Curiosity and inquiry are fostered in an environment in which the child's personal interests and well being play a significant role in the teaching and learning process. As a teacher who believes strongly in educating the whole child, I have witnessed the rapid and immense growth of so many children as I focused on their social, emotional, and personal development, as well as their academic success. My role as an educator encompasses that of a coach, supporter, facilitator and enabler and I believe that it is my responsibility to think of my students, not only as learners but also as children, explorers, and global citizens. It is my responsibility to provide opportunities for students to ignite and engage their whole self. It is through this lens that I have been interested in holistic education.

In this chapter, I will discuss the ways in which I teach holistically in an International Baccalaureate (IB) class. Through an explanation of inquiry-based teaching and learning, whole teaching orientations and transdisciplinary curriculum planning, I will demonstrate how I put the transaction orientation into practice and will unpack some of the corresponding conceptual ideas as they relate to my classroom. In order to paint a clear picture of what my approach looks like in practice I will introduce to you Tai, an imaginary grade four student. The short narrative scenes, woven throughout this chapter, will describe Tai's learning experiences, add a classroom context, and hopefully a deeper, embodied understanding of my holistic teaching and learning approaches.

I have spent the majority of my teaching career working in International Baccalaureate (IB) World schools. The IB is a nonprofit educational foundation that offers programs that "help develop the intellectual, personal, emotional, and social skills to live, learn, and work in a rapidly globalizing world" (IBO, 2013). The IB's mission is to create a better and more peaceful world through education. One of the main reasons that I choose to work in schools that offer the IB's Primary Years Programme (PYP) is because the program is committed to transdisciplinary teaching and learning. The IB states,

> It is also recognized that educating students in a set of isolated subject areas, while necessary, is not sufficient. Of equal importance is the need to acquire skills in context, and to explore content that is relevant to students, and transcends the boundaries of the traditional subjects.

"To be truly educated, a student must also make connections across the disciplines, discover ways to integrate the separate subjects, and ultimately relate what they learn to life" (Boyer 1995). Ernest Boyer proposed that students explore a set of themes that represents shared human experiences such as "response to aesthetics" and "membership in groups." He referred to these as "core commonalities." Boyer's work has been seminal to the development of the PYP. (International Baccalaureate Organization, 2009, p. 11)

Influenced by Boyer's work, the PYP has centered its inquiry on six common themes. These are called the transdisciplinary themes, and each of the six units of inquiry explored throughout the year fall under one of these themes. For example, one of the themes is Sharing the Planet and another is How the World Works. The themes are meant to be globally significant for all students in all cultures and offer opportunities to explore commonalities of human experience. They are revisited each year of schooling, so that the end result is an immersion in broad-ranging, in-depth, articulated curriculum content. The six transdisciplinary themes, "are supported by knowledge, concepts and skills from the traditional subject areas but utilizes them in ways that transcend the confines of these subjects, thereby contributing to a transdisciplinary model of teaching and learning" (IBO, 2009, p. 11). Through this approach I emphasize concept-based, rather than content-based learning, which sets the stage for classroom inquiry.

INQUIRY-BASED TEACHING AND LEARNING

In education, inquiry is often defined as the exploration and discovery of knowledge, skills, and understanding through questioning: "Inquiry implies involvement that leads to understanding. Furthermore, involvement in learning implies possessing skills and attitudes that permit you to seek resolutions to questions and issues while you construct new knowledge" (Szalavitz, 2004). The IBO further defines inquiry by stating that it "allows each student's understanding of the world to develop in a manner and at a rate that is unique to the student" (IBO, 2009, p. 29).

In my classroom, inquiry takes on many different forms since people make sense of the world around them in many different ways. I create opportunities for my students to explore and discover, inside and outside the classroom—on the playground, in the dining hall, in the learning garden, at our outdoor education centre, and in the community. I have worked hard to strengthen my questioning skills in order to better facilitate student inquiry and ask purposeful questions to encourage students to wonder and investigate. I believe that the ultimate goal of inquiry-based learning is to inspire awe and wonder, and this is also one of the goals of holistic education (Miller 2012). Imagine Tai as he experiences inquiry:

Tai loves being in the learning garden. He tells people, "My brain thinks best out here." Today, he and his small group of classmates are busy investigating the idea of communicating without words. They are exploring in the learning garden in an attempt to answer this question: "How do things in nature communicate their needs?"

The questions I ask are open-ended and can often be interpreted in different ways. They encourage thinking rather than a quick or correct response, in an attempt to emphasize that it is the *finding out* rather than the *knowing* that is really valuable. Through questioning I aim to guide learning without restricting it and to foster a culture of inquiry with my students.

WHOLE TEACHING APPROACHES

Along with a culture of inquiry I strive to create a culture of inclusiveness in my classroom by using a balance of educational orientations. Learners make sense of the world around them in a variety of ways, and so it is necessary to use a variety of pedagogical approaches. To reach the whole child, I combine the transmission (when I give students information directly), transaction (when I create opportunities for inquiry-based learning), and transformation (when students connect holistically, and find fulfillment in their own learning) orientations in my own teaching. However, I often use the transaction orientation in our inquiry-based program, as I ask students to "solve a problem or pursue some form of inquiry" (Miller 2007, p. 11).

While Tai is working in the learning garden another group of his classmates are creating a way to communicate an important message to the rest of the class without using words.

Students are often engaged in collecting information, analyzing that information, and drawing conclusions based on what they have discovered. My students also experience learning that is rooted in the transformation position, which gives them the opportunity to make authentic and meaningful personal connections with their learning. They play and work creatively, cooperatively, and artistically. I enjoy bringing drama into the classroom as I find that it helps many students to explore ideas freely and make deeper connections.

I also use the transmission orientation for sharing information, teaching skills, and assessing knowledge. When I am able to create a balance between these three orientations in a lesson, a day, or a unit, I know that I have given students the opportunity to engage the whole self in their learning experience rather than engaging only a part of themselves.

TRANSDISCIPLINARY CURRICULUM PLANNING

In my classroom, a transdisciplinary, concept-based approach to curriculum planning drives my teaching. I plan collaboratively with other grade-level teachers and with a variety of specialist teachers to find ways to integrate different disciplines or elements of the curriculum into single learning engagements. We work to integrate as many subjects as possible around the unit, using each discipline to unpack the Central Idea. All inquiry is focused around this concept-based single statement that "leads to substantial and enduring learning" (IBO, 2009, p. 29) in different ways. There are no blocks for individual subjects such as math, language arts or geography, on my timetable. Instead, all homeroom time is scheduled as classroom inquiry.

> In order to develop a deeper understanding of our Central Idea, "Our need to share our feelings and ideas drives us to develop effective ways to communicate," Tai is involved in a transdisciplinary learning engagement. Key objectives in language, math and social studies are explored as Tai develops, carries out, and analyzes a survey about the use of a modern communication system of his choosing.

This does not mean that we do not have single subject lessons, as sometimes it is important to teach skills in isolation. However, it is necessary to have the flexibility in our schedule to respond to the needs and flow of the class rather than stopping an engaging investigation because the clock tells us that it is time for spelling.

> As Tai is carrying out his survey about the use of social networking, the issue arises that some modern forms of communication seem to be growing at the expense of more traditional forms of communication. Many of Tai's classmates start talking about this so we take the discussion to the carpet, and, as a whole class, we begin to debate the pros and cons of this issue.

It is important that we offer students the time they need to make connections and develop deep understandings of the issues we explore.

I feel that it is also important that there is flexibility in the units of inquiry so that each class's inquiry may go in a slightly different direction, depending on the background knowledge and interests of the members of the class. As long as the teacher's plan follows the same transdisciplinary theme, as well as Key Concepts, Central Idea, and Lines of Inquiry (IBO, 2009), it is not necessary that each grade-level class explore the same content, engage in the same activities and complete the same assessment tasks. Students are involved in curriculum planning and development by asking questions, which lead to sub-themes for our inquiry.

After learning about semaphore flags as a nonverbal communication system, Tai asks, "Why don't we use that system today?" This student-initiated question drives us to inquire into the historical and present day uses of this communication system. We end up exploring why semaphore flags have been replaced with other communication methods and why it's still an appropriate system in certain circumstances. We also make connections between semaphore flags and other communication systems that have undergone similar historical change. The other grade four class does not inquire into this topic in the depth that we do, but explores other topics driven by their own student-initiated questions. Tai is really excited about this part of our inquiry since it stemmed from his question. His excitement and interest leads to student-initiated action and he brings in a newspaper article entitled, "Semaphore and smoke signals—faster than broadband?" This action generates even more discussion about ancient versus modern communication systems.

When students are involved in this process they feel genuine ownership, interest, and purpose in their learning.

A common misconception about inquiry is that it is unstructured, it offers the student too much free rein, and it leads to chaotic classrooms. The truth is that it is quite the opposite. Although inquiry-based learning is flexible, as it responds to the interests and curiosities of the learners, inquiry is also structured, thoughtful, and planned. When planning for a new inquiry I first establish a Central Idea that is engaging, relevant, challenging, and globally significant (IBO, 2009, p. 14). Six weeks of transdisciplinary inquiry will be based around this single statement. Next, I use a backward-design approach, first establishing the outcomes or the Enduring Understandings that I want my students to take away from the inquiry. Then, I identify some of the ways that students might demonstrate their understanding of the Central Idea through a summative task near the end of the unit. After that I look at ways to drive student inquiry through various learning engagements, provocations, and activities.

When presenting students with a new idea or issue we first explore a key question. We spend a significant amount of time brainstorming, exploring, and discussing what we already know so that I can plan based on students' prior knowledge.

In the first few days of this new unit of inquiry, Tai was fairly quiet when we brainstormed ideas for the following teacher question, "Which communication systems do we use in our daily life?" Through our discussions it became clear that the concept of a "system" needed to be unpacked. He already had a lot of knowledge about electronic or technological systems, but this unit of inquiry would offer him an opportunity to learn more about other types of communication systems.

This initial discussion leads to student-led questions, which are recorded, posted in the classroom, and guide my planning for the next steps of our investigation.

After a classmate suggests "body language" as a way to communicate, Tai asks if body language means the same thing in different countries. He says he thinks it doesn't and makes a personal connection by sharing a story about body language that he didn't understand when his family visited Japan. We record his question, "How does body language differ around the world?" and post it on our unit of inquiry board in the classroom.

At all stages of the inquiry process students are encouraged to ask questions, and we work as a team to make discoveries that will answer these questions. It is not the role of the teacher to be the guardian of knowledge and information, but it is the role of the teacher to guide the inquiry and create opportunities for students to ask, discover, and then ask some more. Throughout the inquiry process students are encouraged to make connections, reflect, and take action based on their learning in an effort to make a difference in their lives in the lives of others. If I succeed at this, students will have made significant connections within a transformative learning experience, these being two of the main pedagogical interests in the field of holistic education.

CHALLENGES

Teaching with elements of holistic education, for example, transdisciplinary curriculum, inquiry-based approaches, and a balance of educational orientations certainly can lead to a variety of challenges. Like many things in life, the biggest barricade to holistic education is a lack of understanding. In my experience, a lot of this misunderstanding is rooted in those who were educated in a very different system, are satisfied with the outcome of their own schooling experience, and, therefore, expect educational practices and approaches to remain the same. This lack of understanding can also come from educators themselves who take on an academic-driven, traditional approach to their role as a teacher. It can be challenging to convince colleagues, parents, and other school community members of the benefits of focusing on students' interests, feelings, and well-being rather than on test scores and exam results.

Many people come into our school, one of the most established independent schools in the country, expecting to see quiet classrooms with rows of desks filled with obedient, test-taking children, "brains on sticks" (Miller, 2012). This is often how rigor and excellence are defined. Many see the purpose of schooling as a way to get into university, a stepping-stone to a high paying professional career. The transmission-focused education that they experienced "worked for them" and is what they expect school to look like. The pressure from parents who feel this way coupled with the extreme focus on outcomes in this result-driven era can lead some school administrators to put pressure on teachers to cover the curriculum in order to raise achievement levels and student success. It seems that there is a lack of understanding about how educating the whole child and letting one learn with their hands and heart, as well as their head, *is* the ultimate in achievement and success.

As I delve deeper into holistic education and learn more about engaging the "head, heart, and hands," I am pleased to discover that many of my own pedagogical interests and the philosophies of the PYP are in line with some of the key principles of this educational approach. I am proud of my attempts to reach the whole child, as well as my achievements in the journey to becoming a more holistically minded educator. Many of the elements of holistic education that I use are based at the curriculum level, creating connections between school subjects and striking a balance between different pedagogical approaches. Using a transdisciplinary approach to planning and teaching has allowed me the opportunity to think a lot about the relationships among the domains of knowledge and in doing so, I have been able to create an inclusive environment, "inviting all students into the learning process, providing a broad range of teaching and learning strategies to reach the whole person" (Miller, 2012). An inquiry-based approach positions student interest as the key component in the teaching and learning program. Nurturing curiosity inspires students to explore, discover, and act: to become passionate about their own learning.

As Abraham Maslow's (1943) hierarchy of needs points out, love, belonging, and esteem are fundamental needs. In an environment that is loving, inclusive, and supportive, students have these basic needs satisfied. They feel safe, and as a result, are able to focus on thinking and learning. Through our thoughtful choice of educational approaches and through fostering a classroom culture of inquiry, we can build learning environments rich with balance, inclusion, and connection, a place in which children can feel safe and believe in themselves; their whole selves.

Once we believe in ourselves, we can risk curiosity, wonder,
spontaneous delight, or any experience that reveals the human spirit

—e.e. cummings

REFERENCES

International Baccalaureate Organization. (2009). *Making the PYP happen: A curriculum framework for international primary education.* Cardiff, Wales: Antony Rowe Ltd.

International Baccalaureate Organization. (2013). *About the International Baccalaureate.* Retrieved from http://www.ibo.org/general/who.cfm

Maslow, A. (1943). Theory of human motivation. *Psychological Review, 50*(4).

Miller, J. P. (2012, July 4). Conceptions of holistic education. *Lecture conducted from OISE*, University of Toronto, Toronto, ON.

Miller, J. P. (2010). *Whole child education*. Toronto: UT Press.

Miller, J. P. (2007). *The holistic curriculum*. Toronto: UT Press.

Szalavitz, M. (2004). Concept to Classroom. *Workshop: Inquiry-based learning*. Retrieved from http://www.thirteen.org/edonline/concept2class/inquiry/index.html.

SECTION II

HOLISTIC PEDAGOGY

CHAPTER 10

PRACTICES THAT FOSTER COMMUNITY AND INTERCONNECTEDNESS

Stephanie Aglipay
University of Toronto

My first teaching position in a public school was undoubtedly a challenging experience. The school is located in what is typically referred to in education as a *high-needs* area. I quickly understood that high needs means that there are complex socioeconomic challenges for the students who attend the school. Additionally, there are emotional challenges that directly affect the teaching and learning within the classroom. I was offered a position in this high needs school and was told that if I wanted the job, I would have to start in the next couple of days.

I found myself entering a grade 5/6 classroom in mid-March. From the first conversation with the principal, I learned that the class was in dire need of stability and consistency. I was a little unsure as to how exactly I would create this stability as the students had already experienced four different teachers that year. I would be their fifth. I did not know what to expect exactly in such a short period of time, but it was an opportunity to teach my own classroom and I was willing to take the chance.

Teaching From the Thinking Heart, pages 85–93

This first rather daunting yet exciting classroom teaching experience informed my initial understanding of holistic education. Even though at the beginning of John P. Miller's course, I possessed a very limited insight into what a holistic approach to learning could achieve in a classroom, I found the curriculum practices appealing. They were aligned with the ways in which I tried to foster community in this first challenging 5/6 classroom. I also understood holistic education as a field that places an emphasis on something that is close to my own heart and values, teaching to the whole child. The whole child is not an empty vessel who is void of knowledge and feelings but is a child who is alive with both heart and soul. Thus, teaching within this understanding moves beyond mechanistic curricular practices and aims to forge connections through touching the heart of both the student and the teacher.

FORMING A CONCEPT OF HOLISTIC EDUCATION

After reflecting on my experiences and readings in Miller's course on holistic curriculum, my understanding of holistic education grew into a much larger image than simply teaching to the whole student. My new understanding of holistic education encompassed teaching practices that:

- Engage the mind so that students learn to think critically and creatively.
- Activate the soul, which enlivens the students' inner life or their creative spark.
- Involve the body through movement, games, music, sports, and meditation (Miller, 2010).

When my perspectives on the field began to broaden, I decided to more deeply examine my understanding of holistic education and the ways in which I implemented activities in the classroom to develop a sense of community and encourage the drawing forward of my students' authentic selves.

Before launching into the life world of the classroom and my teaching practices, I will formulate my present concept of holistic education. Miller (2007) gives a concise and comprehensive definition in his book, *The Holistic Curriculum*: "Holistic education is concerned with connections in human experience: connections between mind and body, between linear and intuitive ways of knowing, between individual and community and between personal self and transpersonal self" (p. 7). This educational field seeks a balance between the part and the whole and aims to make meaningful connections between people, subjects, body, soul, and nature: "...the student examines these relationships so that he or she gains both an awareness of them and the skills necessary to transform the relationships where appropriate" (p. 13). One of the most important relationships for a child in school is the relationship between herself (himself) and the classroom community (Miller, 2007). Nurturing connections and relationships within the classroom is so vitally important to learning. Through my first grade 5/6 teaching experience, I learned that connections are strengthened through cooperative learning.

INTERCONNECTIONS IN THE CLASSROOM

Learning Circles

An inclusive learning environment requires having students feel as if they are a meaningful part of a classroom community. To create this interconnected atmosphere, I use learning circles. The circle is a symbol of unity and oneness. The physical aspect of a circle provides a way for each student to look at one another and hold themselves and others responsible. More importantly, when sharing occurs, everyone in the circle becomes a witness to the feelings and authentic nature of each person. Miller (2007) writes that the circle has origins in indigenous communities. A talking stick or object is passed to each person when it is his or her turn to speak (Anderson, 1998). Everyone, therefore, has a chance to be heard and to voice his or her ideas.

Indigenous people view life as holistic. A whole person includes the physical, the mental, the emotional, and the spiritual. At the end of each week, my classroom holds a community circle. It is here where we develop a better understanding of one another as we share our personal views and reveal hidden talents or interests. The community circle is also a familiar activity in classrooms that adopt the Tribes teaching and learning practices. Jeanne Gibbs (1987) developed Tribes as a way to build a collaborative learning environment in which the whole child can be nurtured. Gibbs uses community circles as a space where students can discuss issues, a lesson, or a topic. While in the circle the students adhere to the four positive Tribes agreements: attentive listening, appreciation, right to pass, and mutual respect.

Within indigenous communities the Medicine Wheel is a symbol for interdependence and a guide for well-being. The Wheel is a reminder that people are ultimately interdependent (Bond, 2004 in Varghese, 2009). For example, each member and all living beings on this planet are both distinct and a part of the larger whole. The Medicine Wheel is divided into four quadrants. Each quadrant represents a different aspect of life: the spiritual, emotional, mental, and physical realms. The quadrant functions independently, yet relates to and connects with the other quadrants. Bond (2004) notes that these four quadrants (or realms) and their positions constitute a balanced approach for dealing with issues concerning education. For example, Varghese (2009) uses the Medicine Wheel as an instructional strategy. The teacher guides the student from the realm of the spiritual to the realm of the physical by using both direct and nontraditional methods of instruction.

Our Community Circle

From the first day I taught the grade 5/6 class, I planned to have a community circle that I hoped would foster a sense of interdependence amongst my students. I was eager to learn more about them and was curious to hear how they would portray themselves in front of their peers. At the end of each week, we all reflected on our learning together and discussed our plans for the weekend. However, it was more than just a mere exchange of information; it was an opportunity to share stories that showed what each person truly valued. The class took time out of a busy school schedule to just listen to each others' voices, feelings, and opinions. The community circle became a safe and caring space that allowed us to be our authentic selves.

Setting up the circle took place the last period of every Friday. The students would push aside the desks and place chairs in the middle of the classroom to create a circle. After the setup, I began giving weekly announcements and then would proceed to share a topic for discussion. During the first community circle, I outlined how each circle would function. If a student was ready to share, they would put up their hand. The discussion would begin with that student. We would go around to each person and carefully listen to what they had to say. Those who were not comfortable sharing had the right to pass. After everyone in the circle contributed, I gave another opportunity for those who passed to speak if they felt ready to share. Next, the students could take the opportunity to ask questions. Our time in the circle showed each member's interests and fostered everyone's ability to listen attentively. Most significantly the circle created important peer connections.

I will never forget our first community circle and the excitement it created. I asked the students to say their name, describe one thing that they liked to do and share an interesting fact that was not known to anyone else. I saw some pretty surprised and animated expressions. The room was filled with energy as the students began talking between themselves. Some looked puzzled; naming one interesting fact that no one would really know needed careful consideration. Each student shared openly and with enthusiasm. When it was my turn to speak, I also contributed to the circle. After each circle, I would thank the students; we would pack up for the day and return the desks to their usual places.

There was no one person that would start. Each person within the circle was valued, even if they were silent. There was a remarkable sense of belonging, which is sometimes hard to explain or describe. This was most surely evidenced in the students' responses. After each community circle, amidst the bustle of moving desks, students began talking to each other about what they shared in the circle. I could see in those moments how the inter-connectedness that was formed during the circle did not just finish at the end of the circle time, but carried over into the students' daily lives. I could also see that the students looked forward to this time together. Every Friday someone would ask, "Ms. Aglipay, are we going to have community circle today?" The circle was a learning experience that they could count on, a safe, enjoyable ritual that remained consistent throughout the rest of the year.

The dynamic within the community circle helped to provide glimpses into the students' inner lives while revealing their raw emotions and feelings. The circle began to represent, as Baldwin (1994) posits, "an agent of societal transformation" (cited in Miller, 2007, p. 151). I believed that a transformation was occurring, because the class started to feel less chaotic and more harmonious. Perhaps, the students felt a growing sense of meaningful direction. Our community became further embodied in each circle, as the students happily gathered and reflected together. They were more interested in their learning, especially learning about and from one another. Although all classroom relationships were not perfect, the bonds we forged during our time together were much more caring and compassionate.

Not all the students thought that this new experience would be a valuable learning activity. A couple expressed concerns that the circle was not going to teach them about math or help them with reading and writing. To address these concerns, I explained the purpose of the circle and as time passed and connections were made, these concerned students too looked forward to gathering together every week. A lot of patience was needed. I had to allow for time to process the changes that I proposed. Through this circle I have learned that nurturing students with care, patience, love, humility, and wholeness becomes ever more important when fostering a safe learning atmosphere (Miller, 2010). I believe that it is only then that students can open up and take risks with their learning.

Cooperative Interactions: The Part and the Whole

During physical education class, we would use the circle to warm up. One student would lead the class in a series of stretches. In unison, each student would copy the leader's movements. All of the students became one moving whole, as they learned one another's gestures. Occasionally, I would skip beginning the class in this way. On those days, I observed that the students were less focused and noted that they did not communicate well with one another. The circle seemed to allow for a focused atmosphere and as it was used in a variety of subjects and settings, the students were reminded that they were responsible to others and that they were part of one caring learning community.

Other ways that interconnections can be established are through coop-erative games. I am an avid believer that cooperative learning activities also increase interdependence. I use games such as The Human Knot and Birth-day Line-up to encourage cooperation throughout the year. As I watch the students engage in these activities, I have noticed the goals of holistic edu-cation evidenced, for example, wisdom and compassion, awe and wonder, happiness, wholeness, and sense of purpose. Miller (2007) describes Roger Johnson and David Johnson's (1994) research on cooperative learning, and how interdependence can be encouraged through positive rewards and en-couragement. At times I believe that this type of enjoyment and positivity is often missing in the classroom. A purely academic and subject-centered curriculum focuses on competition and individual achievement, leaving little room for these cooperative activities and the good feeling they bring. Every time I have used a cooperative game in my classroom, I notice that my students are visibly smiling, laughing, and enjoying themselves while authentically communicating with one another.

DEVELOPING THE WHOLE CHILD

While it has been my purpose to create an interconnected classroom through the use of community learning circles, I have also introduced a series of cur-ricular activities that contribute to the development of the whole child, that af-firm the child's authentic self and his or her capacity to resolve feelings within a group. These daily, seemingly insignificant activities remind me how important it is to continue to balance curriculum goals with the development of the whole child. Miller (2007) explains that educating the whole child includes acknowl-edging the soul. He provides detailed perspectives on the soul from a diverse range of religions and psychologists. In short, the soul is "our deeper sense of self" (Miller, 2007, p. 14). I would like to introduce ways in which I nurture the soul through visualization, emotional awareness, and breathing.

Visualization

I typically introduce visualization during subjects such as language arts, visual arts, and social skills (conflict resolution). Visualization can be intro-duced just before journal writing. Each student closes their eyes, if they feel comfortable to do so. I ask them to imagine what they would do for a day if they could do anything, go anywhere, and be with anyone they desired. My goal is to stimulate the students' imaginations, at the same time develop a sense of comfort as they write about something that is meaningful.

Students are often very excited to write about their imaginary day. I feel that their writing is authentic and their responses come from deep within who they are. One student imagined a whole day at the beach with her family in Newfoundland. She wrote that after they enjoyed the beach, the family ate her grandmother's delicious clam chowder. Another student's journal entry described spending the day with her mom, sister, and dad. Her father is often away for long periods of time for work reasons. Another student, newly arrived in Canada, imagined spending the day at Disneyland with her friends and family. This visualization technique provided a springboard for enthusiastic journal writing. The students were becoming more connected to their writing and even though we were drawing on the imagination and visualization, journal entries were genuine expressions of who these students were.

Emotional Awareness

No matter what level of interconnectedness has been established, it is hard to imagine twenty-eight unique individuals getting along throughout an entire day. For conflict resolution, I often do a visualization exercise where I ask students to picture a time when they recall feeling really angry. After doing this practice for a while, I noticed that students were developing awareness to how anger felt in the body as well as when and how they became angry. The next step in the process was to help the students learn ways in which they could calm down and gain insight into how anger influences their actions.

During the visualization, I asked each student to remain silent and to focus on his or her emotions and senses. Students sit in a circle so that they can see the drawing of a body that I provide for their reference. After giving them some time to reflect, I ask the students to describe how their body felt when they were angry. I illustrate their descriptions on the appropriate part of the chart paper body. Students often say that their cheeks feel hot when they are angry, and so I will then color the cheeks red. To conclude this activity the class discusses how we can recognize anger as it rises in the body and mind and ways that de-escalate reactions to these intense feelings. It is important to help students become more aware of their emotions and specifically how they are felt in the body. We often want to tell students to just "calm down" when anger builds, but students need to first recognize their body's reaction.

Breathing Deeply

Another effective technique for coping with anger is breathing deeply. I quickly realized that breathing deeply helps students to focus and feel more relaxed. I will often ask students to take a deep breath if they feel angry or anxious, especially before explaining to me the conflict or argument. I have asked them to do this whenever they are feeling upset or in conflict with someone. A focus on the breath provides the time that the student needs to collect their thoughts and become aware of their actions. When calmer, they can articulate how they feel more clearly. Taking the time to pause allows students to become aware of conflict before impulsive emotional reactions emerge.

CONCLUDING THOUGHTS

The relationships we create with our students play a significant role in establishing the type of coherent community that we as teachers want within our classroom. Engaging students in community circles produces a whole class experience that provides the student time to witness the development of their inner self and the experiences of others. Creating opportunities to participate in interactive and peer-building activities allows students to connect with each other, happily, while affirming a positive relationship to the classroom as a whole. Introducing students to visualization, meditation, and emotional awareness activities reveals my commitment to accessing the heart and thinking of the whole child. Although my first class represented to me an awesome responsibility and was extremely challenging, the activities and the students' reactions showed that holistic teaching and learning practices are well needed in any classroom. All of these experiences can be distilled to one essential statement: Holistic education represents an opportunity for students to become who they truly are within an inclusive and interconnected learning community.

REFERENCES

Anderson, K. (1998). Building the circle. *Adult Learning, 10*(1), p. 21.

Bond, R. (2004). Combating cultural imperialism in Canada: A new role for adult educators? In: J. Satterthwaite, E. Atkinson, & W. Martin (Eds.), *Educational counter-cultures confrontations, imagines, vision* (pp. 69–83). Sterling, VA: Trentham.

Baldwin, C. (1994). *Calling the circle: The first and future culture.* Newberg, OR: Swan-Raven & Co.

Gibbs. J. (2006). *Reaching all by creating tribes learning communities.* Windsor, CA: CenterSource Systems.

Gibbs, J. (1987). *Tribes: A process for social development and cooperative learning.* Windsor, CA: CenterSource Publications.

Johnson, R. T., & Johnson, D. W. (1994). An overview of cooperative learning. In J. Thousand, A. Villa, & A. Nevin (Eds), *Creativity and collaborative learning* (pp. 1–23). Baltimore: Brookes Press.

Miller, J. (2007). *The holistic curriculum.* Toronto: UT Press.

Miller, J. (2010). *Whole child education.* Toronto: UT Press.

Varghese, T. (2009). Teaching mathematics with a holistic approach. *International Journal of Inclusive Education. 13*(1), pp. 13–22.

CHAPTER 11

SOULFUL PHYSICAL EDUCATION

Peggy Donahue
University of Toronto

At 14 years old, I knew that I wanted to be a physical education (PE) teacher. By the time I finished grade 12, there was no doubt in my mind that I wanted to study PE so that I could share my passion for physical activity with future generations. As a student, I had wonderful experiences in my physical education classes and, well, simply any sport I played. Whether it was tag in the gymnasium or a hockey game with my rep team, I could not get enough physical activity. My elementary school teachers, although not formally trained in PE, kept classes in the gymnasium active, challenging, and fun. I remember with fondness, how my grades 7 and 8 PE teacher, Mr. MacKernan, was the resident sports-enthusiast and coach. Although he put us through our paces, all the while he encouraged us and demanded that we give our absolute best. It was also not long before I warmed to my high school PE teacher, Mr. Mullins, with his no-nonsense approach to teaching, his passion for sport, or any kind of physical activity and his dry sense of humor. There was something about my experience in this subject that went deeper than my experience in other subjects. In PE class, I felt alive, genuinely content and connected to myself.

Teaching From the Thinking Heart, pages 95–102
Copyright © 2014 by Information Age Publishing
All rights of reproduction in any form reserved.

Coupled with my passion for sports, physical education classes allowed me to develop skills, think tactically, and play. Body and mind come together effortlessly during play. Play allows me to experience my soul, which means I feel invigorated, free, and yet captivated by the power coming from within. Miller (2000) defines soul as: "A deep and vital energy that gives meaning and direction to our lives" (p. 9). Physical education and sport permit me to simply *be*—to move, to think, and to feel connected to my inner self, without judgment or concerted effort. As Miller (2000) states, "We can recognize soul in people when we see their eyes light up, when their speech is animated, when their body moves with grace and energy" (p. 25).

I am not sure my movements were ever very graceful, but during PE, that "deep and vital energy" rushed through my body. I felt confident, happy, and excited to the extent that I came to know that play is an expression of the soul. During play it is more likely that the individual moves and interacts with objects and others innately and authentically. Being playful reminds us that often children interact with their environment naturally and organically. Play flows from the participant—who moves precisely and strategically, yet without mental anguish, fear of failure or apprehension. As a student, I felt that physical education was a holistic learning experience; it allowed me to experience my mind, body, and soul through a spirit of play.

MAPPING THE DISCUSSION'S MOVEMENTS

I currently teach PE at the junior, intermediate, and senior levels, which has allowed me to develop insight into a broad range of developmental stages. Having experienced my soul though participation in PE and sport, I recognize the awesome potential and power this subject brings to students. If all students are permitted to have soulful experiences, where they feel that deep and dynamic energy, then I believe that it will improve the likelihood that they will go on to lead physically active lives. Carrying forward the ability to enjoy lifelong activity is one of the important goals of physical education.

There are many students who do not experience this vital energy during PE. They simply feel too distressed. Their sometimes-debilitating emotional response is directly related to the daunting task of mastering difficult physical skills. This motivates me to explore the notion of a more soulful PE learning experience. This chapter will present changes in curriculum content, evaluation methods and it will also present mindfulness practices to illustrate how holistic learning may occur in physical education. I am introducing curriculum practices that help students make soulful connections, foster a playful experimental attitude, and reflect on the self as they develop an awareness of the body.

PROPOSING THE NEED FOR SOULFUL CONNECTIONS

To increase the chance of students achieving lifelong participation in sport or physical activity, teachers must revisit how they teach PE curriculum content. This proposed holistic approach to PE, I argue, is becoming increasingly important, as the percentage of students who lack physical activity time is on the rise. Research by Active Healthy Kids Canada (2012) reports that 46% of students have only three hours of active play per week and 63% of school-aged children's free time is spent being sedentary. Daily Physical Activity (a 2005 Ministry of Education mandated twenty minutes of physical activity by all K–8 students per day), compulsory physical education throughout elementary school, and one mandatory credit at the secondary level, are just a few initiatives that attempt to improve the health and well-being of children and youth. It is unclear, however, if these strategies are inspiring students to lead active lives.

The Ontario Health and Physical Education curriculum at both the elementary and secondary levels is organized into strands. While the strands cover Health and Physical topics, there is a significant emphasis placed on developing a wide variety of physical skills for the purpose of enjoying lifelong physical activity. This begins in the primary grades with motor skills (running, hopping, balance, etc.) and progresses into more task and sport specific skills in the intermediate and senior levels.

The content to reach these goals is not prescribed; it is left to the teacher to determine. In the primary grades, students develop movement competence by exploring balance, locomotion, and dance through a variety of experiential activities; these activities are inherently playful. For example, students move like a kangaroo, or blow like a tree in the wind. Typically, around the junior level, this experiential approach is abandoned as PE teachers teach movement competence through the use of individual sport units, and these units focus on skills, rules, and strategies. This approach does little to bring about a true sense of play.

This method uses demonstrations, verbal cues, and corrective feedback to help students master skills. The difficulty with this is that the mind is not truly focused on the body's actions or positioning, but is instead concerned with "looking the part" or executing skills perfectly—the student is not connected to what they are doing. This narrowed focus on successful performance inadvertently shuts out the soul, which shines when one exists, or in this case, moves and interacts freely without fear of judgment or failure. This method also widens the divide between experienced athletes and their counterparts, making soulful experiences very unlikely for the less experienced participants.

While DPA is a commendable strategy, many of the initiatives to get young people moving seem like a band-aid solution as they fail to address what is causing a lack of physical activity. If students' physical activities authentically engage them, for example if they experience a heightened awareness of their bodies, perform actions playfully or through experimentation and see the meaning in what they are doing, their chances of accessing the soul are greatly amplified. As the statistics indicate, there is a responsibility now, more than ever, for PE teachers to embrace a holistic approach to teaching physical education, so that students experience that "deep and vital energy" and continue to enjoy physical activity regularly.

ACCESSING VITAL ENERGY

The following section will describe specific curricular activities that both develop PE skills and ensure that the soul is present during the student's learning experience. As I have mentioned, I believe that the soul is meaningfully engaged when there is choice and when activities are playful and experimental. Instead of dividing the curriculum into separate sport units, physical skills can be delivered according to the TGFU model, which organizes sports into groups based on strategies and fundamental movements. For example, Invasion/Territory games include basketball, football, hockey, lacrosse, and others, all of which have the objective of outscoring the opponent by maintaining possession of the game's object (ball, puck, disc) and invading the opponent's territory. Within each group of games (invasion/territory; net/wall; striking/fielding; target), there are common skills and tactics used which allow the student to apply their understanding and basic skills to a variety of activities. For example, Invasion/Territory games employ the basic offensive strategy of maintaining possession of the game's object and trying to get into an advantageous position to score points. Therefore, teaching students to think about how to position their body to protect and move the object towards the scoring point is transferable between games. Using lead up games (games with simplified rules, skills, objectives, and team sizes) creates a more playful environment. Students can drop their guard and play in the moment regardless of their ability.

Although the goal is, nevertheless, for the student to demonstrate movement competence through sport specific skills (often there are similarities within categories), if transferable skills are emphasized (ones that are repeated in a variety of activities) then this, most importantly, will add to their success and enjoyment of physical activity in the future. Hopper (1998) supports this approach, stating: "TGFU suggests a way of enabling learners to appreciate the joy of game playing that leads to a desire to learn techniques to improve game performance" (p. 4). Hopper articulates my point, concentrating on *how* content is presented and structured can lead to significant gains in learning and greater meaning for students.

Also important to the PE content changes that I am proposing is a more improvisational approach to dance. Although very natural at the younger ages, students become more self-conscious of their movements as they near their teen years. I believe that dance, in its free form, is an expression of the body and mind, and can access the soul. The dance unit in my grade 7 class is comprised of three hip-hop classes taught by a guest instructor. Although appreciative of this reprieve from my own awkwardness, I know there are many students who lack confidence in dance and struggle through the choreography. In addition to traditional dance instruction, this year I incorporated a group dance component where students worked together to choose a piece of music and design a movement sequence. The dance did not have to conform to a traditional dance style, but did have to demonstrate the elements of a good dance, these being: synchronicity, timing, and personality.

Although all of the groups presented a traditional form of dance, the mix of new and previously learned moves, the original music and elements of personality (costumes, facial expressions, and body language) resulted in a performance that was considerably different from a rote dance routine. Each student moved in relation to the group, and to the music, with a sense of comfort. By allowing students to choose the appropriate level of challenge (in terms of dance moves and speed, thereby affecting synchronicity and timing), it eliminated a considerable amount of stress that otherwise would have hindered the nondancers. One of my student's brave declarations at the beginning of the unit was uniformly adopted and manifested by nondancers in the final presentation: "I'm not very good at it, but I like to dance." This statement suggests soulful dance, where one can dance without worry, even if it is in front of the class.

Another example that comes to mind is from a grade 10 co-ed skating/ ice hockey unit. I placed the students in pairs and asked them to develop an "ice dance" to music. I was sure to explain to the co-ed class (who had a wide variety of skating abilities) that the dance was a creative task that involved movement and music on ice. Some students chose to use hockey sticks and pucks, while others, including a pairing of elite male hockey players, opted to perform an ice dance with pirouettes, jumps, and edge work. The class seemed to enjoy the process and everyone smiled and cheered during the final presentation, even for the group that wobbled as they danced on the spot. The more physical education teachers can do to remove the traditional expectations of complicated and flawless choreography and include student choice, the more likely the students are to engage in soulful or playful dance.

MEANINGFUL EVALUATION METHODS

Implementing a soulful PE program naturally requires changes in evaluation practices. It is important that teachers move away from standards-based tests and specific skill performances. I was shocked to hear my niece explain to me that her final grade 9 PE test was based on a series of scores from fitness tests. Equally unacceptable is the practice of measuring skill through quantitative scores (for example, the number of basketball free throws scored out of ten shots). If the overall curricular goal is to create life-long participation in sport and/or physical activity, then evaluation methods must move away from the mastery of skills.

In harmony with the soulful content suggestions, I would like to present two evaluation tools, which focus on meaningful experiences and student voice. Portfolios (I have used video-based) can be employed to demonstrate students' progress and development of skills. Incorporating self-assessments and reflections enable all students to achieve success. If the emphasis for evaluating students shifts from absolute mastery to student selected mastery and student development, then students will be more equipped with the confidence and positive experience they need to enable them to engage in lifelong physical activities.

I have witnessed the firsthand benefits of changing my evaluation practices to better meet the needs of all students through the use of videos. My colleague and I created videos that showed us performing skills incorrectly and we asked students to identify and correct the errors in the performance, through a written response. This method gave students an equal chance to demonstrate their understanding and to apply their knowledge. Students were thrilled to provide feedback on how to correct the movements and made insightful suggestions on how to adjust these skills in game settings.

The use of a personal scrapbook assignment is another evaluation method that embraces student choice, reflection, and personal connection. *The Legacy Project*, by Nancy Zigovic (Miller, 2010), provided some of the inspiration behind this assignment. The scrapbook is a compilation of journals, interviews, and reflections that are related to physical activity. One memorable assignment required the students to lead a physical activity that engaged the whole family. I read entries on family walks, shinny and dodge ball games, tobogganing outings, and many others, all of which suggested a playful experience.

There is one entry that sticks out in my mind as a particularly strong example of a soulful experience. My student wrote about the success she had leading her family through a dance class in the living room. Initially the family was hesitant but by the end of her activity, they were suggesting that it become a weekly activity. It was evident that soul, in its capacity to share and connect, emerged through the simple act of one family member playfully sharing her love of dance with the rest of the family. Parents repeatedly told my colleague and me that the scrapbook was a topic of discussion in their homes—the students were genuinely interested and excited by its challenges. This yearlong assignment gives students an opportunity to reflect, engage, and explore physical activities of their choosing. The scrapbook assignment draws attention to the activities that students find playful and meaningful—activities that engage the soul.

AWARENESS OF THE BODY

The final suggestion to bring about holistic or soulful learning in PE is through mindfulness. Miller (2010) defines mindfulness as "being present in the activities we perform from moment to moment" (p. 101). The subject matter lends itself very well to mindfulness, with its demanding combination of physical skills and mental acuity. Most often, students are provided with verbal directions and visual demonstrations for skills and then asked to practice and perform them. Students go through the motions without complete focus because they have not been coached on how to be more mindful or aware of their physical movements. Their performances lack that deep conscious connection that leads to meaningful learning. PE teachers must make an effort to teach their students how to perform physical activity mindfully.

Students need coaching in mindfulness and the use of specific techniques can be employed by teachers to achieve this. For example, giving students time to feel the sensations in their bodies internally and allowing them time to slow down while attending to the moment are simple practices that can be implemented any time during physical activity. In addition to demonstrations and explanations of body positions, students also need to make use of kinesthesia (awareness of the position and movement of the parts of the body by means of sensory organs in the muscles and joints). Students need to be more cognizant of the dynamic physical and energetic changes that occur in the body during exercise. For example, when demonstrating the overhand volleyball serve in the starting phase, the teacher would draw the students' attention to the sensation of a strong stretching feeling in the shoulder ligaments. This form of attention leads to a heightened awareness within the body. Kinesthetic learning requires a moment of full attention, of mindfulness, to enhance a student's sensitivity to the feeling of the movement. Examples such as this one and others that make use of body positioning and energetic awareness will assist students, not only in developing their technique, but also in strengthening connections between the body and the mind.

This kind of consciousness is also relevant to practicing yoga, but is largely neglected during other physical activities in PE. Mindfulness can also be integrated through the use of short meditations. Walking students through a body scan at the beginning of class will help them identify what areas they need to focus on during stretching. Short yoga and breathing practices can help the student feel present in their bodies while remaining calm and connected to their inner selves.

The use of visualization is another way to draw students' attention to the present moment. Miller (2000) identifies visualization as a tool for "activating the inner life of a student" (p. 63). Visualization, already popular in elite sports, can easily be adapted to physical education. Gaylean found that increased attention, confidence, and relaxation are some of the positive effects that visualization can have on students (as cited in Miller, 2010, p. 74).

CONCLUDING THOUGHTS

On the surface, a soulful physical education class might appear no different from a traditional one—students move, develop appropriate skills, and remain on task. When I attend to my class more closely, however, I see that the students who are engaged in soulful physical education display noticeable differences: a bounce in their step, an air of self-confidence, and a genuine connection to and presence within their actions. The soulful PE teacher has intentionally interwoven the principles of playful learning, personal meaning, experimentation, and awareness into their content, evaluation methods, and teaching practices to both deepen and elevate their students' experiences. Students carry these powerful experiences forward, enabling them to lead active lives well into the future.

REFERENCES

Active Healthy Kids Canada. (2012). *Report card on physical activity for children and youth.* Retrieved from: http://dvqdas9jty7g6.cloudfront.net/reportcards2012/AHKC%202012%20-%20Report%20Card%20Short%20Form%20-%20FINAL.pdf

Hopper, T. (1998). Teaching games for understanding using progressive principles of play. *CAPHERD (27)*1, 1–5. http://education2.uvic.ca/Faculty/thopper/WEB/Cahperd/principle.pdf

Miller, J. P. (2000). *Education and the soul.* Albany: State University of New York Press.

Miller, J. P. (2010). *Whole child education.* Toronto: University of Toronto Press.

CHAPTER 12

NURTURING THE WHOLE CHILD

Is it Possible in a Public School Setting?

Jennifer Forsythe
University of Toronto

ME, MY CLASSROOM, AND HOLISTIC EDUCATION

I am a teacher, a wife, and a mother of two. I have been teaching in Toronto for 13 years and have taught junior kindergarten, up to and including grade 5. I began my studies and career in the field of Early Childhood
Education. When I worked with the youngest of students, I often felt like
more of a caregiver than a teacher. The caregiving part of my day mir-
rored what I was doing as a parent, but over time and with reflection, I
was able to identify how the teaching and parenting of children are two
very different things.

My colleagues and myself are definitely caregivers as well as educators.
My students do not come from privileged families. Many of their parents
are new Canadians struggling to find work. The children live in high-
rise apartment buildings, surrounded by busy roads. They live with their
grandparents, aunts, uncles, and cousins, often sharing a bed if they have

a bed to sleep in at all. The children make use of the breakfast program as well as the snack program provided by the school. We regularly buy food and clothing items for children in need, with our own money. We dedicate many hours after school listening to parents and helping them access community resources that seem complicated and overwhelming to many families. I identify the caregiving of my students as providing them with what they need to survive, to get through the day without feeling uncomfortable or hungry. But the role of the teacher must go deeper than that.

Regardless of our efforts to provide for basic needs, to create a safe learning environment, as well as our attempts to address the unique needs of parents, can we truly claim that public school teachers are deeply nurturing the whole child? Nurturing is bigger than giving care. Nurturing the whole child is to instill a sense of wonder in the world around them, allowing children to question and explore their place in the cosmos. As we concentrate on filling our students' minds with information we cannot ignore the hearts and souls of the young people we are trusted with each day. It is true that our school days revolve around delivering information, but how do we deliver it? Are we structuring our days in a way which students will be prepared for and open to the new information?

In order to begin this discussion about nurturing the whole child in public schools, I will present my own assertions regarding what it means to nurture the whole child:

- A nurturing classroom allows children to feel as well as think.
- The teacher has a responsibility to provide space and time for students to come to their own conclusions through experimentation, contemplation, and physical experiences.
- Teachers need to facilitate earth connections, allowing students to see themselves within the largest possible context, the cosmos (Miller, 2007, p. 163).
- I believe the soul has a place in the classroom. When I refer to soul I mean the true self, not just the assumed societal role we hold, be that male, female, son, or daughter.
- Teachers must be willing to acknowledge their own hearts and souls if we are going to foster our students' awareness of their own true selves.

In this chapter I will describe the teaching practices that I implement to develop a caring and nurturing classroom community. I will discuss how to develop true curriculum connections for our students as well as how to instill caring, mindful relationships with the earth and with each other.

NURTURING A CARING CLASSROOM COMMUNITY

As stated in *Whole Child Education* (Miller, 2010), "fundamental to reaching the whole child is providing a caring community" (p. 62). Very early in my career I learned the value of sharing my true self with my students and I quickly learned how that practice created a greater evidence of kindness, caring, empathy, and honesty.

In my first few years of teaching, I thought there was a certain way teachers were to interact with their students. Unfortunately that belief made me feel like I was "acting" like a teacher all day. Once I allowed myself to be truly present, to be the me I am when I am at home or walking down the street, I instantly enjoyed my work day more and felt truer connections to the students I spent so many hours with each day. I now tell them honestly when I am feeling frustrated with their behavior or if I am happy about something that is happening in my life. When they see me as a real, feeling, loving person they are more open to sharing their own true selves with me.

I instill the notion that we are like a family; in fact we spend more time with one another than we do with our own families. This sense of family within the classroom allows for a feeling of belonging and safety. I want my students to truly know and believe that we need to show love and kindness to one another. I welcome each child with a smile and a personal greeting every morning. In return, they say good morning to me and ask about my family. We are genuinely happy to see one another each day. When particular students and their difficult behaviors overwhelm me, I try to remind myself to revisit my relationship with them and make some time to reconnect with them to ensure a continued positive relationship. It is always worth the effort.

Community Circles

Every morning, our community circle is a time to observe the mandatory schoolwide routines, such as O Canada and the morning announcements. The circle allows for a time to sit together and to take note of how each of us in the room is feeling. Sitting in a circle, as opposed to all my students facing me, allows us to start our day as a whole unit. We are all present to one another. The children are encouraged to share how they are feeling as well as if they have had any experiences since we last gathered. Many children are keen to immediately share the most intimate thoughts and feelings. Others may not share until late June. I make sure to share how I am feeling, good or bad. This gathering allows me to hear right at the beginning of the day, if there is someone who didn't get to eat breakfast or if they had an argument at home that is still lingering with them. This circle time could potentially be viewed as wasting time through the eyes of another. Colleagues have expressed that belief to me. I know in many class-rooms students begin the day with "bell work," an attempt to squeeze as much academics into the day as possible. If time is used well all throughout the school day, I believe there is plenty of time to meet my academic goals for the students as well as for community building activities.

Our community circle does not exclusively happen at the beginning of the day; there are frequently moments when we gather in our circle to discuss events that arise throughout the school day such as conflicts at recess or hurt feelings. Students will request a circle time when they have something they wish to work through with the entire group. Last year one of my students asked for a community circle to help solve a problem she was faced with. She was overwhelmed by the fact that a student in a different class consistently targeted one of her classmates at recess. Her classmate needed help and she wanted us to work together to make things better. I may not have known this was happening at all, if she had not requested the circle. She wanted us to come up with ways that the children in our class could support the child being bullied. Together we did role-play activities which gave the students the words and confidence to know what to say when they need to stand up to someone. The students made a group decision to ensure that the targeted student always had a buddy at recess. With my gentle facilitation and through allowing the circle time to be a part of our routine, the students handled this situation brilliantly.

NURTURING CURRICULUM CONNECTIONS

Within the area of curriculum I believe there are three main concepts to consider when programming for students. In order to nurture good thinkers and strong problem solvers we need to:

- Group our lessons under broad themes or big ideas.
- Allow for incubation time after delivering new information.
- Be creative in how we deliver new information.

Big Ideas

Within the Toronto District School Board there has been a push for a number of years to integrate subject areas. The message from the Toronto District School Board's instructional leaders is that more curriculum content can be taught if we integrate the subjects. As stated in *The Holistic Curriculum* (Miller, 2007): "If we can relate subject matter to the inner life of the child, subjects become less abstract and more relevant. It is also important to explore connections between subjects" (p. 131). Recently I have learned how to teach content under the umbrella of a theme or Big Idea.

At our school we have divided the year into quarters, each quarter has its Big Idea. One of the most successful Big Ideas has been social justice. Under the theme of social justice we are able to explore issues that are local, personal, and global. We write, read books, and consider our social studies and science content all through the lens of social justice. Allowing for the children to see how the information within the curriculum works together on a broader scale provides them with the opportunity to discover, "the oneness of things" (Miller, 2010, p. 47). Students learn to connect to one another, to the past, and to people around the world by coming to know concretely what social justice means and how we all have a role in making it a reality.

Incubation Time

By incubation, I mean the time to sit with new concepts and think them through. This process is like allowing new information to grow strong roots in the mind, a chance to become permanent, not just words that are heard and left to float away. Incubation requires time and in our public school classrooms, time is often what we feel we are lacking. It is hard to imagine having your class sit quietly, maybe with their eyes closed and the lights off for any amount of time. Often I have seen classes like this when they are being disciplined for being too loud or rambunctious. I have had to teach my class that being silent does not mean that they are in trouble. Students need to be guided as to what to do when they are sitting in silence. They can be guided as to how to keep a piece of information in their minds and make the internal connections to it. If a story has just been read, leave the students with a question to quietly ponder: How would you have responded if you were the main character? We often have children prove their thinking on paper and we need to leave that behind sometimes. Incubation time is giving them the time to formulate their own ideas and questions internally. This is a life skill that will create the thinkers and problem solvers of the future.

Creative Delivery

If you work with children you know that there are some no-fail ways to get their attention and to spark their interest in the information you are presenting to them. Some of these strategies include music, drama, visual arts, and technology. If it is my goal to not only deliver the content to my students but to also spark a sense of curiosity and wonder in them, I need to be creative about it. For knowledge to take hold in a child's mind or for imagination and wonder to be ignited, the students need many different opportunities to experience new information. Children can learn mathematic concepts through physical activity, or science through visual arts. Social studies can come to life through a dramatic interpretation. As stated in *The Holistic Curriculum* (Miller, 2007), drama and dance can "help the student connect the mind and body" and "by connecting mind and body we facilitate wholeness" (p. 128). It is that wholeness that comes from a nurturing classroom.

NURTURING EARTH CONNECTIONS

Environmental education has always been of great importance to me. I was raised to appreciate our earth, the water, plants, and the sunsets we see each night. I am now raising my own children with a respect for the planet by talking about the natural world and their place in it, by appreciating time outside, and mostly by being aware of nature whenever and wherever we are, whether we are on a city street or in a massive forest. I am trying to do the same in my classroom. Miller (2007) states:

> Earth connections can reawaken us to the natural processes of life. The wind, the sun, the trees, and grass can help us be alive and awaken us. As much as possible, students should have direct experiences with the earth through such activities as gardening, caring for animals, and outdoor education. (p. 68)

I believe in my heart that there are simple yet powerful ways to foster earth connections including the simple notion that children need to be outside. They need to breathe the outside air, feel the warm sun or cold wind on their faces. They need to have soil under their feet not just concrete or tile floors. My school is fortunate to have a large grassy playground. I see how the children are refreshed and energized after a vigorous recess playtime. I make an effort to get the students outside at other times of the day as well, to read, conduct an outdoor science investigation, or have an art class. Spending any amount of time outdoors is energizing for both my students and me. It prepares us all for better concentration and alertness when we are back inside the building. Making my inner city students aware of the nature that surrounds them every day is a gift I can give to both them and to the planet. Taking a moment to watch a squirrel busy at work or to watch the clouds moving and changing above us is worth the time it takes.

Our students are more likely to grow up to be guardians of the earth if they have made a connection to it as a child.

This past year we took our grade 4 and 5 students to an outdoor education centre for three days and two nights. I believe there were moments over those three days when the students' hearts and minds were awakened to a place they had never known before. They fed chickadees from their hands. They went on a night walk without flashlights and on that walk they learned through direct experience how the human eye naturally adjusts to meet our needs when the only light is the moon. They saw stars they never knew existed. The teachers connected with our students on that trip in a way that allowed for success throughout the school year. We are going again this year and I know it will be well worth the effort and sacrifice of being away from my own family for those days.

NURTURING MINDFULNESS IN THE CLASSROOM

One of the results of mindfulness practice is that teachers tend to be less reactive in the classroom. When a student's behavior is challenging to the teacher, mindfulness helps the teacher process what is happening in a more spacious manner rather than immediately reacting. Often the immediate reaction can be something the teacher later regrets. (Miller, 2010, p. 103)

My students are faced with many challenges each day, including hunger, sleeplessness as well as anger and frustration. Each year I have a number of children who have a difficult time maintaining the behavior that is necessary and expected of them in school. When I practice mindfulness I am able to be present for the children who need me the most. In the first week of school this year I was completely overwhelmed. I had over thirty students, many with a variety of outstanding needs. My own children were having a difficult transition from summer freedom to the back to school routine. I remember one moment sitting in front of my class; they were being really noisy, distracted, and completely consuming. I had to center myself in that moment and focus on my breathing. I centered my mind and pushed away the stress of the chaos and time pressure. When I felt ready and calm I was easily able to gain the students' attention and to guide them through the same process I had just worked through inside myself. We were all feeling the same way; they needed me to be mindful so I could be patient with them and have empathy for their stress level and uneasiness. Continuing to create the spaciousness that mindfulness offers, I need to change the pace of my entire day. I need to simply slow things down, be present and mindful of the small moments and aware of how the stress of daily life may be clouding my ability to nurture myself and my family.

CONCLUSION: NURTURING THE THINKING HEART

I am convinced that it is possible to not only care for and teach my students in a public school but that I can truly nurture the children I work with each day. If we as teachers look at the task we are given with an open heart and clear mind, the obstacles to a nurturing classroom are surmountable. We must be willing to have potentially difficult conversations with our administrators when questioned about our actions. We must be prepared to justify what might at first glance appear to be a classroom in which nothing is happening because the moment is a silent and still moment. We need those moments to pause for contemplation, incubation, reflection, and mindfulness.

A teacher who allows his or her thinking heart to guide them in the classroom is a teacher who makes decisions for his or her students based on core beliefs about what children truly need, not simply based on the prescribed curriculum. We need to open up dialogues about creating caring classroom communities, curriculum connections, earth connections, and mindfulness with teachers, parents, and administrators. I absolutely can create a nurturing classroom in a public school setting. As each new year begins, I endeavor to take on the challenges of curriculum and timetabling and the never ending lists of things to do with a thinking heart and calm and centered mind.

REFERENCES

Miller, J. P. (2007). *The holistic curriculum.* (2nd ed.). Toronto: University of Toronto Press.

Miller, J. P. (2010). *Whole child education.* Toronto: University of Toronto Press.

CHAPTER 13

FROM TRANSACTION
TO TRANSFORMATION

A reflection on Previous Professional
Experience in EFL Course Design

Ahmed Kandil
University of Toronto

A few years ago, I was given the chance to write an Integrated Skills Course
(ISC) for students studying in a language institute in an affluent Arab country. The students were between the ages of 16 and 21, and they studied EFL
in that institute after they had successfully completed grade 9. The program
was skills-based, wherein the students studied reading, writing, and communication skills in three discrete courses. This idea of teaching one skill at
a time in a language course was dubbed by many as the atomistic perspective of language learning. In other words, that second language learning is
the sum of its parts, thus students should learn by focusing on these parts
one at a time. In reaction to this criticism and in order to create balance
in the English language program, it was decided to use Task-Based Language Learning (TBLL) as one of two main theoretical frameworks for the

Teaching From the Thinking Heart, pages 111–118
Copyright © 2014 by Information Age Publishing
All rights of reproduction in any form reserved.

ISC course. In TBLL, students acquire knowledge and skills as a result of completing a certain number of tasks and/or projects, which constitute the content of the course. The other framework was Computer Assisted Language Learning (CALL) because the course was taught in the computer lab where computers and Internet could be used to facilitate instruction and the completion of the tasks and projects. In addition to the EFL program, students studied other subjects such as math, science, and various technical subjects depending on their area of specialization. Upon graduation, students were awarded a technical high school diploma that enabled them to work as technicians in the oil and gas industry of that country.

The Integrated Skills Course (ISC) course was basically a series of tasks and projects that culminated in a product, such as an essay describing the entire process; a PowerPoint presentation to be given in class; a brochure to be used in an awareness raising campaign; or an Internet site showcasing students' work. The course required students to work cooperatively in pairs and/or groups and use the language skills (reading, writing, listening, and speaking) plus technological skills (e.g., using the computer, browsing the Internet, typing, and using various software programs) in order to complete authentic or pedagogic projects. The choice of the projects was negotiated with the instructor at the beginning of the school year in order to make sure that schoolwork was relevant and meaningful for the students. The completion of each project took between one and three weeks of ongoing individual, pair, and group work inside the computer lab and out of class as well.

Generally speaking, students' motivation was the biggest challenge for most of the instructors. A large number of the students came from well-off families, and they repeatedly stated that they were studying at the institute because their parents "forced" them to. Otherwise, they would not have made that choice themselves. Virtually all the students were local citizens of that affluent Arab country with a relatively small population (a few million people) and whose economy is based on crude oil production. What's more, the number of expats working in that country is comparable to the size of the local population. In this context, local citizens occupied most of the mid- and high-level managing jobs while the "foreigners" occupied virtually all other kinds of jobs. Many of the youngsters in that country felt they did not have to work since they were receiving good money from the government and from their families. Many of the students, then, viewed the degree as a social convenience required of them by their families. In this context, it was fundamental to initiate themes for projects that resonated with the students and provide them with an incentive to complete the tasks of their choice. Some of the themes suggested for the course included travel, buying a new car, designing a dream house, and choosing a career that was compatible with their talents and skills.

This brief description of the course, the students, and the educational and sociocultural contexts is necessary before reflecting on and re-evaluating my course design experience.

GENERAL CRITIQUE
AND RE-EVALUATION OF THE COURSE

With regard to holistic education, the above-mentioned EFL course included the following elements.

1. The course required students to use the various language skills cohesively in order to complete meaningful tasks and projects. This approach was different from teaching each language skill separately in a discrete course, e.g., grammar, writing, and/or reading courses.
2. Students had regular input into the course especially at the beginning of the school year when they suggested which projects to work on. The projects were therefore meaningful and relevant for the students, which reflected positively on their attitude and improved their motivation.
3. Assessment was more authentic, as it was not simply based on a pencil and paper test that students took at the end of the year. Instead, students passed the course if they satisfactorily completed the various stages of the project and submitted a final product that genuinely reflected their own efforts. In doing so, the focus was predominantly on the process rather than the product.
4. The course involved the principles of cooperative learning, as students usually worked in pairs and/or groups to complete their projects. Each student had a role to play, and the completion of the project required each student to contribute to the group and work collaboratively with group members. Overall, this created a positive classroom community and a lively work environment.
5. In hindsight, I think there were three interwoven strands that had a huge impact on the planning and the design of the ISC. The first strand was incorporating the principles of communicative language teaching as delineated by scholars such as (Bell, 2003; Canale & Swain, 1980; Kumaravadivelu, 2001; Nunan, 1999; Oxford, 1997; Richards & Rodgers, 2001; Savignon, 1991; Tudor, 2001). The second strand was integrating the elements of task-based language learning (TBLL) as advocated by Long, 1994; Pica, 2005; and Skehan, 2003. TBLL was viewed as the vehicle that would enable the students to connect the various language skills in a cohesive and authentic manner. The final strand that had an impact on the course

was implementing the basic principles of course design (e.g., needs analysis; selection, sequencing, and gradation of materials; collection of feedback from teachers and students; students' assessment; and course evaluation; Cotterall, 2000; Graves, 2000; Nunan, 1988, 1989; Richards, 2001).

REVISION

If I were given the chance to revise the ISC for a second edition, I would pay particular attention to the following points:

1. Subject Connections: I would support the current skills-connections aspect of the course by subject connections. One way to do this would be to connect the various subjects through major relevant themes, for example pollution. Such themes would encourage students to investigate various strands in diverse subjects (e.g., geography, history, science, and mathematics) in order to come up with solutions to some problems that are posed throughout the study process. This would enrich the educational process and make study more relevant for the students. In addition, such framework would enable the instructors to detect and nurture talents students possess in the diverse educational, social, academic, and artistic domains. Further, connecting subjects will empower teachers to develop the course from an interdisciplinary to a transdisciplinary orientation and, consequently, from transactional to transformational education.

2. Intercultural Competence: I would include the theme of intercultural competence (ICC) as advocated by scholars such as Alptekin, 2002; Bennett, 2004; Byram & Feng, 2004; Byram, Gribkova, & Starkey, 2002; Byram, 2008; and Levy, 2007. Making better use of the huge IT capabilities available in the institute and pairing my students with students from other parts of the world would encourage students to explore varied cultures. Bennett's (2004) Developmental Model of Intercultural Sensitivity (DMIS) should be of great help in this regard, as it helps students move from ethnocentrism (where students see themselves and their own culture as the center of the universe) to ethnorelativism (where students learn that culture is diverse, dynamic, multilayered, and socially constructed). The overall goal of the ICC theme would be to help students realize they are not alone in this world and train them to reflect on other people and cultures from an emic versus etic perspective. To help students reach this level of understanding, other people's cultures should be tackled not only at the surface level (e.g., historical highlights and

tourist attractions) but also at a deeper level (e.g., people's customs, traditions, and belief systems). Such a study of the vast cultural tapestry should provide students with inter- and intracultural awareness.

3. Earth Connections: I would highlight earth connections by introducing nature and ecology into education projects. The idea is to help students see the earth and all beings on it as one indivisible whole, and that one change in any part will have an impact on that whole. One particular example that comes to mind is the pollution and garbage problem that local media in that country constantly highlight. The local authorities in that region were concerned about the unprecedented level of pollution that struck their environment at levels higher than those of other countries that had much larger population. In particular, they lamented the fact that pollution was even creeping into the desert, which is very dear to the local population due to their Bedouin heritage. This theme and students' genuine interest in the desert could be exploited so as to have the students probe the pollution problem by having them read about it, investigate it further, collect facts and information about it, meet representatives of local authorities, conduct field trips, interview local residents, and propose some solutions to that problem. Such an approach should create a stronger connection between students and nature in a way that highlights unity and wholeness as underlying principles in the universe.

4. Spirituality: I would introduce strategies such as visualization, metaphors, journals, mindfulness, body–mind connections, and meditation in order to create a course for the inner life (Miller, 2007, 2010). One particular strategy that comes to mind is storytelling and the use of local literature to introduce important concepts that are not properly tackled through the linear scientific thinking model. One value that such an approach could lead to is nurturing and tapping into students' wisdom, which is defined by Miller (2007) as "intelligence rooted in the soul. The ancients call this the 'thinking heart.' Wisdom links intuition and intelligence in order to deal with the large questions: What is our role in the universe? How can we deal with human suffering" (pp. 25, 26)? Using storytelling in addition to local, ancient, and universal literatures to address such big questions would strengthen students' imagination and intuition and create an excellent balance with the overdose of linear and scientific thinking instruction that students are exposed to in our modern-day education. In addition, such an approach would help students reflect on their own identities and place the identity construct at the core of the learning process as suggested by Cummins (2001) and Norton (2006). It is noteworthy to indicate that without spirituality

my revision of the course would be wholistic and not holistic, as this quote suggests: "Holistic is sometimes spelled as 'wholistic.' I do not use the words interchangeably, but suggest that 'holistic' implies spirituality, or a sense of the sacred, while 'wholistic' is more material and biological with an emphasis on physical and social interconnection" (Miller, 2007, p. 6). A spiritual component, thus, would be one important requirement to make sure the course is truly holistic and not just technically wholistic.

5. Community Connections: I would highlight community connections not only at the classroom level through cooperative learning and community of practice (Wenger, 1998), but also at the larger level by getting students involved in projects in their own neighborhoods and/or towns. One project to introduce would request students to investigate the difficulties that some expatriate workers encounter as outsiders. If students get the chance to meet these people, interview them, and hear their perspectives face-to-face, they will most probably develop a sense of empathy and an ability to see the world from other people's perspective. Such empathy would also enable the instructor to introduce the concept of legitimate peripheral participation (Lave & Wenger, 1991) so that students can understand that such poor workers have the right to participate in the various activities in their community even if this participation is peripheral in some social aspects. I believe it is such educational experiences that will help students become ego-relative and self-introspective. It will also help them see human beings as part of one whole community, so the sufferings of some people in that community will have an impact on people everywhere. Human beings, like everything else in the universe, are interdependent regardless of their religions, ethnicities, or social status.

The suggestions above will be a building block towards educating the whole student, as the changes made in only one area cannot turn the entire school into a holistic one. What I have suggested for course revision so far is more of cornerstones or principles that I would incorporate (rather than a prescriptive account of how to transform one subject into a holistic one). The reason is that:

> Educating the whole child needs whole teaching, a whole curriculum, whole schools, and whole teachers. Although whole child education challenges administrators and teachers, it can help create schools where students enjoy being and learning. The aim of whole child education is the development of children and adolescents who can think, feel, and act and whose bodies and souls are nourished. (Miller, 2010, p. 13)

Finally, I would like to conclude this paper by stating that the principles, knowledge, and insight I have gained from studying "The Holistic Curriculum" helped me to revise my educational philosophy, moving away from one that was fragmented, and to pay more attention to the linguistic aspect of students' education toward a more holistic vision. My new vision thus is to help my students grow holistically as balanced individuals who have great potential as well as responsibility towards themselves, their smaller community (family, friends, school, neighborhood) and their larger community (country, region, and the planet). I will do that by facilitating my students' environment and education in order to empower them to achieve their full potential and shoulder their responsibilities across all domains. In doing so, I will always keep in mind that change is gradual, organic, and dynamic (vs. linear and lockstep). I will always instill in my students a sense of reverence for life, interdependence, and interconnectedness so that they see themselves, their communities, and the entire universe with its incredible diversity as one indivisible whole. Love, care, patience, presence, and humility will always be the principles upon which I base this vision. Meditation and mindfulness will be two important tools I will always use to renew my energy and my commitment towards myself, my profession, my students, and all beings everywhere.

REFERENCES

Cummins, J. (2001). *Negotiating identities: Education for empowerment in a diverse society.* (2nd ed.). Los Angeles, California: California Association for Bilingual Education.

Graves, K. (2000). *Designing language courses: A guide for teachers.* Boston: Heinle & Heinle.

Kumaravadivelu, B. (2001). Toward a postmethod pedagogy. *TESOL Quarterly* *35*(4), 537–560.

Lave, J., & Wenger, E. (1991). *Situated learning: Legitimate peripheral participation.* Cambridge: Cambridge University Press.

Levy, M. (2007). Culture, culture learning and new technologies: Towards a pedagogical framework. *Language Learning & Technology, 11*(2), 104–127.

Long, M. (1994). On the advocacy of the task-based syllabus. *TESOL Quarterly, 28,* 782–795.

Miller, J. (2007). *The holistic curriculum.* Toronto, Canada: University of Toronto Press.

Miller, J. (2010). *Whole child education.* Toronto, Canada: University of Toronto Press.

Norton, B. (2006). Identity as a sociocultural construct in second language research. *TESOL in Context [Special Issue],* 22–33.

Nunan, D. (1988). *Syllabus design.* Oxford, UK: Oxford University Press.

Nunan, D. (1989). Toward a collaborative approach to curriculum development: A case study. *TESOL Quarterly, 23,* 9–25.

Nunan, D. (1999). *Second language teaching & learning.* Boston: Heinle & Heinle.

Oxford, R. L. (1997). Cooperative learning, collaborative learning, and interaction: Three communicative strands in the language classroom. *The Modern Language Journal, 81,* 443–456.

Pica, T. (2005). Classroom learning, teaching, and research: A task-based perspective. *Modern Language Journal, 89*(3), 339–352.

Richards, J. C. (2001). *Curriculum development in language teaching.* Cambridge, UK: Cambridge University Press.

Richards, J., & Rodgers, T. (2001). *Approaches and methods in language Teaching.* (2nd ed.). Cambridge: Cambridge University Press.

Savignon, S. J. (1991). Communicative language teaching: State of the art. *TESOL Quarterly, 25*(2), 261–277.

Skehan, P. (2003). Task-based instruction. *Language Teaching, 36*(1), 1–14.

Tudor, I. (2001). *The dynamic of the language classroom.* Cambridge: CUP

Wenger, E. (1998). *Communities of practice: Learning, meaning, and identity.* Cambridge: Cambridge University Press.

CHAPTER 14

THE HOLISTIC CLASSROOM PROJECT

Preparing for a Teaching Year That Focuses on the Pursuit of Happiness, the Power of Empathy, and the Exhilaration of Being Present

Grant Minkhorst
University of Toronto

INTRODUCTION

I will be the first to admit that in the past, I had a tendency to be cynical about anything that screamed "self-help." I associated self-help materials with weakness and low self-esteem. But over the past year, my tune has changed. This change occurred slowly and with a certain degree of pragmatism and analysis. After reading numerous articles and books and attending a fair share of lectures, I arrived at the conclusion that "self-help" has little correlation with weakness or low self-esteem. Self-help is synonymous with growth.

Teaching From the Thinking Heart, pages 119–129

If the title of this paper seems familiar, it should. It was adapted from Gretchen Rubin's 2009 book, *The Happiness Project*. Rubin's book intrigued me for a variety of reasons. First, the idea of happiness has captivated me due to its subjectivity and abstractness. Second, I have tried to incorporate the pursuit of happiness into my teaching practices. Rubin's book is a recounting and analysis of her yearlong journey to be happier. Inspired by Rubin's book, as well as Eckhart Tolle's, *A New Earth* (2005) and Mary Gordon's, *Roots of Empathy* (2005), I embarked on a mission to plan an entire school year around the ideas of happiness, empathy, and being present.

I have named the mission *The Holistic Classroom Project* because I believe that happiness, empathy, and being present are the three pillars of holistic education. While the three basic principles of holistic education are balance, inclusion, and connection (Miller, 2007), happiness, empathy, and being present, I believe, can facilitate both the three basic principles of holistic education as well as provide a practical framework for instructional strategies, student assessment, and daily routines in the classroom itself.

In the afterword, I have included a brief description and reflection on the *The Holistic Classroom Project* as it materialized during its first attempt. As with any new endeavor, there are bound to be challenges and roadblocks along the way and this journey was no different. As frustrating and exhausting as my experiences were during the implementation process, the learning and professional growth reminds me that, not only was it worth it, it was also utterly transformative and, for that, I am grateful.

DESCRIPTION AND RATIONALE

The Holistic Classroom Project was borne out of my desire to teach the whole child to allow her to see her own place in the universe and the world and begin to help her gain a sense of purpose (Miller, 2010). By laying out my three pillars (happiness, empathy, and being present), I am hoping to have a framework for designing specific objectives, lessons, activities, and assessments.

Modeled after the plan in Rubin's, *The Happiness Project* (2009), I have divided the school year into three sections, each spanning approximately three months. Each section will focus on one of my three pillars. Section 1 will focus on the pursuit of happiness, Section 2 on the power of empathy, and Section 3 on the exhilaration of being yourself. Never having tried anything like this before, the sequence of the pillars was more of a gut-feeling organization than something grounded in research and analysis. Starting with *happiness* seemed to be the most logical entry point, as it should allow me to form bonds with my students through learning about their interests and passions. *Empathy* came next, as it is my hope that, after being a third of the way through the year, my students will have formed the bonds necessary to care about each other and thus place more value on the idea of being empathic. Finishing the project with *being present* just felt right. By this point in the year, my class has usually turned from a collection of random students to a community of peers. Focusing on *being present* will require the commitment of the entire class and this is more likely at the end of the year when strong connections have been established and nurtured.

This paper will lay out my rationale for each section, complete with opportunities and challenges. As with any project, it will be subject to many revisions, additions, and illuminations. It is my hope that *The Holistic Classroom Project* will be a starting point for a new kind of teaching, one that practically incorporates holistic education into the pedagogy of teachers everywhere. But I would like to just start with one teacher: me.

SECTION 1: THE PURSUIT OF HAPPINESS

Unhappiness covers up your natural state
of well-being and inner peace, the source of true happiness
—Tolle, 2005

Being happy is not as easy as switching on a light switch. Scoffham and Barnes (2011) write, "Happiness matters. It matters so much that many of us make personal fulfillment and well-being the main aim in our lives" (p. 535). One of the fathers of positive psychology, Mihaly Csikszentmihalyi, believes that a joyful life is the creation of the individual, one that cannot be copied (1990). If this is the case, which I believe it is, then one of the teacher's main responsibilities should be to facilitate learning that brings each student joy, or what Csikszentmihalyi calls *flow*. Reaching *flow* is when one is so absorbed in an activity or task that time seems to fly and the ego disappears, or when challenge and skill intersect (Csikszentmihalyi, 1990). My classroom should be a place full of students in a state of *flow*.

Being a middle school teacher, adolescents present different opportunities and challenges from those students in the younger grades. Csikszentmihalyi and Reed (1984) assert that, "Teenagers are maddeningly self-centered, yet capable of impressive feats of altruism" (p. xiii). Based on this assumption, beginning the project with happiness would allow my students to be a little self-centered before tapping into their altruism for Section 2 (empathy).

Fredrickson's (2000) "broaden-and-build theory," suggests that happiness and elation broaden our thought-action repertoire and allow us to build psychological resources. Building these psychological resources would be vital for Sections 2 & 3 of the project on empathy and being present.

Providing opportunities for happiness and elation is the first priority for the project and "teachers are in a strong position to construct interpersonal and physical environments which are likely to generate flow experiences" (Scoffham & Barnes, 2011, p. 541). It is my intention to construct these conducive environments that empower my students to engage in learning activities that generate high levels of happiness and flow. The first three months of the school year will provide students with multiple opportunities to explore areas of their own interests and passions. The students, in collaboration with myself and a select group of peers, will design their individual learning units with a focus on learning goals, curriculum connections, and formative and summative assessments.

With an increasing number of children reporting lower levels of satisfaction with school (Currie et al., 2005), teachers are wise to engage their students in activities that maximize their happiness and state of *flow*. It is my hope that Section 1 of the project accomplishes, and exceeds, the goal of optimal student engagement happiness, and flow.

SECTION 2: THE POWER OF EMPATHY

You do not become good by trying to be good, but by finding the goodness that is already within you, and allowing that goodness to emerge.
—Tolle, 2005

Bullying continues to be a massive problem in schools around the world (Nansel et al., 2001). With bullying behavior peaking in middle school (U.S. Department of Education, 1998), I wanted to address the issue head-on in Section 2 of the project. This section will focus on using the power of empathy to: (a) decrease bullying; (b) increase student connectedness; and (c) facilitate the growth of an inclusive classroom environment.

Empathy has the power to act as a force that enables us to embrace our inherent connectedness and compassion. Miller (2010) writes that, "If we see ourselves as connected to others, then the compassion arises naturally since we do not see ourselves as separate from other beings" (p. 30). By making *the power of empathy* the focus for Section 2 of the project, cultivating empathic behaviors in students will act as the framework around which all activities, routines, and assessments will revolve.

Stacey Stanbury's 2005 study found that by enacting programs that build confidence and empathy, facilitated by counselor and teacher assistance, schools can decrease bullying behavior. While my current school already uses programs that focus on empathy and confidence (Tribes, Kelso's Choice), I wanted to explore a new program with a different approach. My exploration led me to Mary Gordon's *Roots of Empathy* program. Gordon's program places *baby* in the role of *teacher*, where empathy is cultivated through an infant's purity, innocence, and radiation of love. As Gordon (2005) explains, "It is a program that has the capacity to instill in our children a concept of themselves as strong and caring individuals, to give them an understanding of empathic parenting and to inspire in them a vision of citizenship that can change the world" (p. 6). The potential of the *Roots of Empathy* program is rooted in its proven ability to facilitate a "celebration of our differences and recognition of the common ground that binds us together as human beings" (Gordon, 2005, p. 144).

The *Roots of Empathy* program will provide a strong companion to the collaborative work we will do as a class. Section 2 of the project will see students engaging in multiple cooperative activities where the importance of understanding differing points of view will be paramount. I intend to use role playing and other drama-based activities in order "to allow students to place themselves in a vulnerable social position without any real threat or danger to themselves" (Fischer & Vander Laan, 2002).

In addition to the use of drama, I will focus on contemplative education strategies outlined in Padmasiri De Silva's 2011 book, *Tolerance and Empathy: Exploring Contemplative Methods in the Classroom*. Silva focuses on two central principles of contemplative education. The first, *deep listening*, takes some of the emphasis off critical listening and replaces it with listening that is open and ungrudging of the other person, where we listen longer than to just formulate our counterargument. The second is the adoption of "a less deliberative and a slower, more intuitive approach to deal with situations more intricate, shadowy, and, at times, seemingly paradoxical," where we "slow down, relax, listen, and respect the flow of life" (p. 100). These contemplative education strategies will involve a variety of self-reflexive practices, the use of the environment, and a concentration on experiential learning. One of the great virtues of contemplative education is that "it does not seek quick answers to questions" (Silva, 2011, p. 101). During this section, students will explore questions that empower them to contemplate the experiences and lives of others, begin to think outside of themselves and learn the great power of empathy.

SECTION 3: THE EXHILARATION OF BEING PRESENT

With seeing comes the power of choice—
the choice of saying yes to the Now, of making it into your friend
—Tolle, 2005

Preparing for a year that is authentically *holistic* should include transformative teaching practices, or teaching that focuses on wisdom, compassion, and sense of purpose in one's life (Miller, 2010). In order to achieve these goals, I will use the first two thirds of the school year to focus on happiness and empathy. However, the final section of the project, *The Exhilaration of Being Present*, I believe, will prove to be its most vital. In the age of ubiquitous technology and distractions, society is increasingly disengaged from the world around them. Tolle (2005) elaborates on the problem when he writes, "The human mind is highly intelligent. Yet it's very intelligence is tainted by madness. Science and technology have magnified the destructive impact that the dysfunction of the human mind has upon the planet, other life-forms, and upon humans themselves" (p. 10). I have seen my students gradually becoming more detached from themselves and the world around them. The education world is also becoming overrun with labels: gradual release, higher-order thinking, balanced literacy, etc. The more we attach these labels to things, the more we become deadened to reality (Tolle, 2005) and, I would argue, the less authentic our learning experiences turn out to be.

The journey of empowering students to "be present" begins with a central idea: Know Thyself. Adopting holistic practices "lets us realize our deeper sense of self, our soul" (Miller, 2007, p. 14). Focusing on the self and the present for the last section of the project will incorporate strengthening connections to five areas: the mind–body, the subject, the community, the earth, and the soul (Miller, 2007). The five areas of connection outlined in Miller's *The Holistic Curriculum* provide the practical framework for the final section of the project.

Human consciousness, while challenging to awaken, provides freedom from the trappings of the ego (Tolle, 2005). As a middle school teacher, I see students who are experiencing constant attacks on their ego. These attacks are manifested in countless ways, from social pressures to the often-treacherous path of establishing their identity. Creating opportunities for my students to connect to themselves and the world around them will be the primary focus of Section 3.

I will begin by helping my students connect to their mind-body and soul. While I intend to begin the practice early in the year, whole class meditation and mindfulness activities will be integral to building these connections. Each day, I will engage the class in a 5–10 minute meditation using a variety of techniques (breath counting, visualization, mantra and movement). We will also begin a "Mindful Minute" at some point throughout each day. This practice has every student work to be completely mindful of the task at hand for just one minute during the day. In order to make subject matter less abstract and more authentic, we will focus on finding connections between the subject matter and ourselves. While the goal seems vague, it is a practice that is already central to my teaching philosophy. I am always engaging my students in activities where finding a connection to the content is the entry point to an authentic learning experience.

In terms of facilitating a community connection, all students will be asked to take part in a project that benefits the community in which they live (i.e., volunteering at a food bank, walking younger students to school, participating in the Environment Club). Students will be asked to reflect on their experience with a particular emphasis on how it helped them build a stronger connection to their community. Finally, creating a connection between student and Earth will be done through spending time outdoors. As a class, we will focus on learning to appreciate our environment and the gifts provided by the earth. We will plant a school garden and learn to tend to it mindfully and patiently.

The final section of the project will present many opportunities and challenges, but its importance is essential to creating a holistic classroom. Tolle (2005) writes

> A vital question to ask yourself frequently is: What is my relationship with the present moment? Then become alert to find out the answer. Am I treating the Now as no more than a means to an end? Do I see it as an obstacle? Am I making it into an enemy? Since the present moment is all you ever have, since Life is inseparable from the Now, what the question really means is: What is my relationship with Life? This question is an excellent way of unmasking the ego in you and bringing you into the state of Presence. (p. 124)

Being present and putting students on the path of "knowing thyself" has the potential to enact growth that will transcend the walls of the classroom and beyond.

CONCLUSION

Holistic education is more than just a teaching philosophy; it is a means to open the doors to understanding humanity, finding life balance, and spiritual enlightenment. Teaching holistically removes the emphasis on covering objectives and constantly establishing and assessing countless learning goals and replaces it with learning which educates the whole child: mind, body, and spirit.

As I embark on this journey, I recognize and welcome the challenges that teaching holistically presents; it is through these challenges that I will grow as a teacher and create ever-more authentic and holistic learning opportunities for my students. As the holistic curriculum is rooted in the presence of the teacher (Miller, 2007), I will aim to be present for my students and for myself. I will engage my mind, body, and spirit in every element of this journey, from the planning stages through to the assessment and reflection.

As an educator, it is my responsibility to ensure my students' wellbeing and development. I think that teachers misinterpret the concepts of wellbeing and development when they only view them through the lens of a standardized curriculum. Miller (2007) writes, "We realize that the final contribution that [the students] make to this planet will be from the deepest part of their being and not just from the skills we teach them" (p. 199). For me, education will always be more than lesson plans, summative assessments, and curriculum standards; it will be about the beauty of fulfillment, the power of connection, and the awesomeness of knowing thyself.

AFTERWORD: A REFLECTION ON THE FIRST ATTEMPT

Like most everything in education, this project proved the oft-cited discrepancy between theory and practice. When I embarked on my year-long journey of creating a holistic classroom, I was walking along the proverbial road paved with best intentions. I planned out my first few weeks in details and sketched out the remainder of the school year.

The first month of this project exceeded my expectations. I was assigned two different classes, one very different from the other. I opened the year with all things positive and engaging. I spent hours meeting with each and every student in my attempt to fully understand their goals, aspirations, and areas of growth. I ate lunch with my students during most days, engaging in conversations to better understand the social dynamics of the class. I made every effort to enter and leave the school every day with a smile and a positive attitude. I soon realized that the obstacles to achieving this constant sunny disposition were large and very, very real.

The central obstacle to creating a holistic school year was the job action recommended by our teacher union. This conflict between teachers and the government complicated many of my plans. It soon became apparent that bringing in outside guests, scheduling clubs and activities at break times, and organizing special activities for our students would not be easy, or even possible.

A second obstacle, which was not one I had anticipated due to the sometimes-insular nature of graduate school, was the reality that I was working with a team of other teachers as part of a strong, cohesive group of intermediate teachers. In my planning, my ideas were classroom-based initiatives, which would be facilitated by me and for my students. The reality was different. I needed to ensure that my teaching partners, many of whose pedagogical experience was greater than my own, were invested in the initiatives that I was originally just proposing for my class, in my classroom. It was evident that I would not be able to achieve all of what I had set out to do if I wanted to maintain a positive and productive relationship with my teaching partners. I would have to pare down my expectations and plans in order to make it work for everyone.

The process of paring down my plans was a necessity for both staff cohesion and also in response to our job action as part of our ongoing dispute with the government over contract negotiations. I decided that I was going to choose a few initiatives from my original plan and make the best of a year fraught with obstacles and challenges.

- Community Circle: As part of our weekly routine, the class would meet for 30-minute "community circles." These weekly meetings were actually designed as part of our board's implementation of the *Tribes* program. These class meetings allowed for both students and teachers to discuss their learnings, goals, and observations throughout the week. The time spent with students during this precious time allowed me, as their teacher, to understand their reality as it was oftentimes different from my vantage point. We used the time to celebrate our successes, deconstruct our challenges and conflicts, and plan for the upcoming week, month, and term. Allotting time that is dedicated to student voice ensured that my students felt valued and appreciated as members of the class community.
- Entrance Interviews: One of the most enjoyable parts of my experiment was my decision to have "entrance interviews" with each student. I slotted approximately 20 minutes to meet with each student to discuss their goals, frustrations, and family situations. I took time to understand where they were coming from so I could more effectively and thoughtfully help plan where they were going. Oftentimes, these interviews would morph into casual conversations about life, school, and the minutiae of smartphone technology (or something similar). I kept all of my notes from these interviews and referred to them constantly. This "collected data" helped me solve countless issues, from punctuality to peer-to-peer conflicts.
- Teambuilding Challenges: The intermediate team dedicates the first two weeks of the school year to developing collaborative and communication skills through a series of team building exercises. These activities blend our grade 7 & 8 students into various teams where they are forced to work together in order to reach a common goal. The goal of each individual activity varies from those which require patience and concentration, to those which include a collaborative physical task. We ensure that these tasks are accessible for all of our students while also prioritizing *learning* over *winning*.
- The Six-Word Memoir: My students' first task of the year is to write, and digitally present, a six-word memoir. The six-word memoir, in summary, is a literacy activity that allows students to deconstruct and

analyse their young lives in deep and meaningful ways. Students are required to write six words which encapsulate the experiences from their lives. This activity proved to be incredibly powerful in that students, through self-reflection and discussion, had to confront the most impactful and formative moments of their lives. This self-actualization activity not only helped my students know themselves better, but it also helped me understand my students beyond a purely surface level.

• Picture Book Read Alouds: As part of my focus on empathy, I made an effort to take my students to the library for a weekly read aloud. I would choose a book with a strong message and central theme which we could discuss before, during, and after reading. Using children's picture books allowed for a light-hearted, yet meaningful, discussion about important themes relevant to them like bullying, fitting in, and family conflict. The discussions that ensued after reading were poignant, engaging, and thoughtful with students often identifying with certain themes or specific characters. The discussions would often spur further conversations about our class community with students making relevant and timely connections from the picture book.

• Journaling: As a forum for self-reflection, each student had both a hardcopy journal and an online blog. They were both designed to help students practice their writing while simultaneously engaging them in self-analysis and thoughtful narratives. There were times when students would be given a specific writing task (i.e., write about your happiest childhood memory) while other times they were free to choose the topic about which to write and explore.

Upon finishing the original paper, I was filled with excitement and anticipation to return to the classroom after a year away pursuing graduate studies. I planned and planned with detail greater than anything I had attempted in my previous eight years in the classroom. But how does that saying go again, "If you want to make God laugh, make a plan"?

I would be lying if I said that I wasn't disappointed in the outcomes of my original plan for a holistic year of learning. But, in reality, my professional learning was richer than I had imagined. This past year proved, like each and every year in the classroom, that flexibility and creativity is the key to student learning. I adapted a rigorous program focused on happiness, empathy, and self-actualization into something manageable and realistic. The loftiness of my original goal of the program (to produce a classroom full of happy, empathetic, and self-actualized students) was probably what forced me to persevere with elements of the program in an otherwise unbearably trying year full of challenges and setbacks.

I look forward to this upcoming September as I try it all over again, but this time with lessons and learning that will benefit my students and help more meaningfully ensure the success of providing a holistic educational experience.

REFERENCES

Csikszentmihalyi, M., & Larson, R. (1984). *Being adolescent: Conflict and growth in the teenage years.* New York, NY: Basic Books.

Csikszentmihalyi, M. (1990). *Flow: The psychology of optimal experience.* New York, NY: Harper and Row.

Fischer, J., & Vander Laan, M. J. (2002). Improving approaches to multicultural education: Teaching empathy through role playing. *Multicultural Education. 9*(4).

Fredrickson, B. L. (2001). The role of positive emotions in positive psychology: The broaden-and-build theory of positive emotions. *American Psychologist, 56*(3), 218–226.

Scoffham, S., & Barnes, J. (2011). Happiness matters: Towards a pedagogy of happiness & well-being, *Curriculum Journal, 22*(4), 535–548.

Stanbury, S. (2008). The eects of an empathy building program on bullying behaviour. *Journal of School Counselling, 7*(2).

Stavrinides, P., Georgiou, S., & Theofanous, V. (2010). Bullying and empathy: A shortterm longitudinal investigation. *Educational Psychology, 30*(7), 793–802.

Tolle, E. (2005). *The new earth.* New York, NY: Penguin.

CHAPTER 15

IDENTITY AND AUTHENTICITY IN THE ESOL (ENGLISH AS A SECOND OR OTHER LANGUAGE) CLASSROOM

Elana Freeman
University of Toronto

Meaningful learning occurs when both teachers and students bring their authentic selves into the classroom. For an adult English Language Learner (ELL), the authentic self can include educational, work, and family history as well as political, religious, racial, ethnic, cultural, and linguistic background. In order to acknowledge them fully, educators working with adult ELL's need to view students "as having a complex social identity and multiple desires" (Norton Pierce, 1995, p. 17). In fact, "when language learners speak, they are not only exchanging information . . . but they are constantly organizing and reorganizing a sense of who they are and how they relate to the social world (Norton Pierce, 1995, p.18). Of course, new experiences in a new country, settlement or otherwise, can shift a learner's sense of self.

This paper will focus on the importance of allowing students to bring their whole selves into English language learning, specifically, by examining the roles that teacher presence, politics and first language play in the classroom. Personal examples of how my own awareness of these roles is shifting, as well as my attempts to implement this knowledge into my teaching context, are addressed.

TEACHER IDENTITY AND PRESENCE

Embracing the idea of multiple identities can assist students in the development of intercultural competence or the ability to interact and communicate openly, effectively, and respectfully (which is an immensely important part of thriving in new country), so educators need to create opportunities for learners to develop these skills by accessing the whole person. In addition, given that intercultural competence is an essential skill for ELL educators to possess in order to do their jobs effectively, they must include themselves within these opportunities, so they can continually develop this skill. The notion of authenticity and multiple identities needs to inform not only how we see our students, but how we view our own identities as teachers as well.

In an attempt to use a learner-centered approach, teachers are not always conscious enough about the way in which their own backgrounds influence classroom dynamics and discussions. In my own experience, a misplaced notion of learner-centeredness led me to neutralize some aspects of my own presence in the classroom. In this respect, my relationship to and openness about my own cultural background in the classroom is an area I have been reassessing in terms of connecting with students in a more authentic manner. Although I have always viewed my students' cultural backgrounds as essential contributing factors in the classroom and to their learning experiences, I have never examined how my own cultural views and assumptions contribute positively or negatively to these experiences, and I have often tried to keep all politics (theirs or mine) out of the picture. I cannot ignore the political element of my presence in any classroom as a white, native speaker of English in a position of authority. I have not yet been able to find my way through the bigger picture of power dynamics in the classroom, and I expect that I will be exploring it throughout my career as a teacher. I have, however, begun to look more closely at it on a more personal level. In an attempt to be apolitical and appear totally neutral, I have always had reservations about acknowledging my Israeli roots since many of my students are from various parts of the Middle East. I have feared any kind of political discussion around such possibly controversial or contentious issues. My less than conscious paranoia about revealing too much of my own background changed when I realized that by asking students to share information about their culture and by keeping mine hidden, I am not only encouraging an inequality in class dynamics, but I am preventing students from creating real and authentic connections with me and each other. This omission can lead to missing out on rich conversations and teaching/learning opportunities, which would bring more meaning to language use for the students.

During a recent teaching term, I took the small conscious step of acknowledging my own cultural background in the hope of connecting with my students in a more transparent way. On the first day of class, I used an introductory activity that was suggested to me by my course lead. The activity concerned names and included questions that students could ask their partner such as: "Do you like your name?" and "What does your name mean?" The students were then to present their partner's answers to the class. As an extension of this activity, I had the students write their names on the board both in English and in their native languages. Although this activity itself is not so far outside the realm of something I would normally do with students, what was different was my decision to begin it by writing my own name in English and in Hebrew, thus, immediately revealing a part of my own cultural identity. By taking this step, many important connections on multiple levels were made. There was a palpable joy and pride for those students writing their names in their first language, and there was curiosity and excitement in observing others write in these new languages with scripts many had never seen before. The students had questions and were delighted to see that I could write my name in another language as well. I even had one student who shared her experiences living in Israel. Another student from Iran asked me how to say "peace" in Hebrew and then said it to me everyday at the end of each class. Yet another student knew a surprising amount about Judaism and shared some of his knowledge with the class. Even though this is not a novel activity in an ESOL classroom, my intentions behind it helped bring about a real awareness of all the connections between culture, language, and identity for me and hopefully for some of my students.

CULTURE INCLUDES POLITICS IN THE CLASSROOM

Acknowledging and incorporating students' cultural backgrounds into the classroom environment and curriculum is key, but the framework for such acknowledgement needs to be expanded and deepened. Like many new TESOL (Teaching of English as a Second or Other Language) professionals, when I first began teaching, I limited my definition of culture to celebrations and equally light subject matter, and I shied away from topics involving differing views and political content. I have come to realize that whether I acknowledge it or not, students bring politically charged experiences with them into the classroom. There are always concerns about the directions political conversations can take, but I am starting to see that these issues are, more often than not, a part of students' identities, and it is necessary for them to feel that they can safely share these thoughts if they wish. In addition, educators must remain aware of their own political lens, so that when political or social issues are addressed in the classroom, students are given space to present their own views. Without proper awareness about one's own perspective, a teacher runs the risk of not recognizing both the need for and validity of other viewpoints.

The type of politically charged experiences that students may carry with them became clear to me when a student in one of my classes shared some of his background. "Ben" (his chosen English name) was a student from China whom I did not get to know well during the teaching term. Prior to our conversation, I knew that his wife was an international student, and it was clear that he was very kind and well liked by many students in the class. He was social with students mainly outside of his own culture. His English skills were quite good overall, and his grades were at the top of the class. Ben struck me as thoughtful and bright. He had a very pleasant personality, but he did not command a strong presence in the classroom. On the last day of class, I let my students leave a bit early, but made myself available for anyone with questions or concerns. Ben stayed behind to speak to me about his listening skills, which were good for the level, but a skill he felt less confident with. We spoke about this and then the topic changed; he began to talk about politics in China.

This was the first time I had ever heard a Chinese student broach this topic. He addressed this same observation by explaining that there is such a strong culture of "saving face" in China, that even if Chinese citizens are aware that there are problems, they will not talk about them. He spoke about the media bans in China, about the lack of freedom of speech, about Tiananmen Square and how he would never speak of such things in front of the other Chinese students in class. He told me about a friend who had been arrested because of his religious beliefs. I asked if it was Falun Gong (a spiritual practice and philosophy involving the meditative movement of qigong, which is banned in China). He told me that he had spent two years in a Chinese prison for being a Falun Gong practitioner. He began to cry. I was under the impression that I was the first person he had told since arriving in Canada (outside of the Falun Gong community in Toronto). We sat and talked, and I felt strongly that Ben didn't want a thing from me, except someone to talk to, and so I listened. This interaction would not have occurred had I not been practicing a kind of mindfulness about my fears and boundaries around difficult subject matter as well as my reservations about becoming a sort of counselor for my students. While I do believe that some boundaries are absolutely necessary, I am rethinking mine and am trying to be more mindful about them.

LANGUAGE AS CULTURE—LANGUAGE AS IDENTITY

Beyond issues of teacher presence and politics in the TESOL profession, another issue relating to identity is that the inseparability of culture and language is not always recognized. In many language programs, this kind of acknowledgement is discouraged due to strict "English Only" policies. For some time, I have been trying to determine an appropriate, effective and balanced way to use first language (L1) knowledge within my teaching context. The name activity icebreaker previously mentioned is a small example of how bringing in the first language (in this case by writing names) can allow for students to make personal connections with each other.

When approaching an adult ESOL classroom, regardless of specific context, we must avoid the conscious or unconscious assumption that adult learners have no useable L1 competencies, since this perpetuates the construct of teacher as locus of all knowledge and student as a passive recipient of information. Indeed, if a student's prior knowledge and linguistic and cultural background is accessed, this allows them to contribute to a class as an equal and to challenge power imbalances (Cummins, 2001). The complete exclusion of a student's first language inside and beyond the classroom runs the risk of sending a message that an important part of who they are is problematic and inhibiting their ability to learn. As a result, I believe this policy not only prevents students from bringing their authentic selves into the classroom, but also hinders teachers from meeting the needs of students. There are multiple studies (Atkinson, 1987, Brooks-Lewis, 2009, Cook, 2001, Cummins, 2001, Osburne, 1986, Piasecka, 1988, Roberts Auerbach, 1993) which show that excluding the L1 can have exactly the opposite affect such policies intend, and that classroom use of an L1 can assist in second language (L2) acquisition.

The question of how to actually implement L1 on a practical, day-to-day basis is not a straightforward one, and I do not advocate L1 being used indiscriminately in the classroom. Measured L1 use in the L2 learning space such as learners using their first language for note-taking during listening exercises, for record keeping, or for the purposes of language analysis can prove helpful to students. Another means of introducing an L1 is to purposefully place students in same-language groups so that they can compare information such as comprehension of a reading, or ideas for a group project. This kind of pairing is often something teachers and even some students avoid, but there is much to recommend strategic use of same-language grouping. Vivian Cook (2001) views the use of the first language during pair work as a natural, valid, and helpful way to facilitate a task. She notes that this can trigger code switching, which "is a normal feature of L2 when the participant share two languages" (p. 418). According to Cook:

There is no reason why students should not code-switch in the classroom. Furthermore...L1 provides scaffolding for the students to help each other.... Through the L1 they may explain the task to one another, negotiate roles they are going to take, or check their understanding or production of language against their peers. (p. 418)

Another possible approach is to ask students to write drafts in their first language and then (without direct translation), have them rewrite in their second language. The idea underlying this activity is that the initial ideas and concepts are formulated much more freely and easily in the L1. It is important to recognize that it is unlikely that all such approaches will be successful in all circumstances, and, accordingly, they should be selected and explored carefully. Ultimately, we can empower ELLs by encouraging conscious utilization of L1 in the classroom, and softening "English Only" policies can allow students to use existing skills to move their learning process forward.

In order to further explore the connection between first language, culture, and their relationship to learning, I have consciously attempted to address this issue in my teaching in an explicit way. For instance, on the first day of a recent term, when I elicited possible classroom rules from my students, several of them brought up the "English Only" rule. I asked students what they thought about this rule, and also explained my view about it. I told them that as long as they were careful and thoughtful about the use of their first language, that existing lingual knowledge has value and is potentially helpful. A few students seemed skeptical, but I could see that most were pleasantly surprised and felt recognized for the knowledge they already possessed. It is interesting to note that the students were respectful and mindful of this new take on the policy throughout the term, and did not simply speak their first language to avoid practicing English (which I have observed when the English only policy is strictly enforced). I witnessed their use of L1's as scaffolding for themselves and each other. In fact, this responsible and conscious use of the first language may have always been the intention of most students in past classes, but the fact that there was no tension around the issue in my classroom made the learning environment more open. I believe that allowing the students to stay connected to such an important part of their identities helped them feel more connected to me, each other, and the learning process.

FINAL THOUGHTS

Identity, particularly cultural identity, is complex, multidimensional, and dynamic. It is influenced by past and present, culture and language, and experience and interaction.

An expanded concept of identity for both teachers and students can provide opportunities for more meaningful connections in the TESOL classroom. Shifting my framework around the issue of identity has allowed me to move closer to an informed practice of promoting student authenticity and a more holistic learning experience. Although many of the ways in which I structure activities (pair work, group work, scaffolding) has remained essentially the same, I now create more opportunities for students to share cultural perspectives in order to foster an atmosphere of understanding. As a result, I have begun to focus more on creating activities that both implicitly and explicitly address language and culture on a deeper level, and to encourage students not only to share and learn from one another but to think critically as well. I plan to remain mindful regarding this expanded approach to authenticity and identity in the classroom which includes politics, first language and my own presence and to implement smaller and larger changes to my teaching to this effect.

REFERENCES

Atkinson, D. (1987). The mother tongue in the classroom: A neglected resource? *ELT Journal, 41*(4), 241–247.

Brooks-Lewis, K. A. (2009). Adult learners' perceptions of the incorporation of their L1 in foreign language teaching and learning. *Applied Linguistics, 30*(2), 216–235.

Cook, V. (2001). Using the first language in the classroom. *Canadian Modern Language Review, 57*(3), 402.

Cummins, J. (2001). *Negotiating Identities: Education for Empowerment in a diverse society* (2nd ed.). Los Angeles, California: California Association for Bilingual.

Norton Peirce, B. (1995). Social identity, investment, and language learning *TESOL Quarterly, 29*(1), 9–31.

Osburne, A. (1986). Using native language writing in the ESOL composition class. *TECFORS, 9*(2), 1–5.

Piasecka, K. (1988). The bilingual teacher in the ESL classroom. In S. Nicholls & E. Hoadley-Maidment (Eds.), *Current issues in teaching English as a second language to adults* (pp. 97–103). London: Edward Arnold.

Roberts Auerbach, E. (1993). Reexamining English only in the ESL classroom, *TESOL Quarterly, 27*(1), 9–32.

CHAPTER 16

FOLLOWING FEELING DURING MIND–BODY INQUIRY

Kelli Nigh
University of Toronto

Tell me what is a thought?
Of what substance is it made?

William Blake

Early Adolescence: A Meditation Circle

Angela, Digby, Isabelle, Rose, Gwendolyn, and Dylan sit in a circle with their hands stretched out, holding them a few inches away from each other. The lights of the drama classroom are dimmed. Drumming music is played. Soft breathing is heard. After three minutes the students describe what they see. Dylan saw gorillas dancing. Isabelle ran through a forest and met a young child. Gwendolyn saw a fire with people dancing. Rose also saw a fire, burning in the midst of a large clearing. Angela said that her hands were tingly. The activity is called a meditation circle, a place to remain open to imaginal experience. This is what happened when the students followed feeling while watching their imaginations.

Teaching From the Thinking Heart, pages 139–148
Copyright © 2014 by Information Age Publishing
All rights of reproduction in any form reserved.

Late Adolescence: A Primal Exploration

The students stand in a circle. The first student enters the circle, makes a sound and gesture, and continues to free the gesture and sound. Choosing another student, the first student teaches the second student to mimic the original sound and gesture. Two bodies are now within the act of becoming one. The first student leaves the second to transform the movement, on their own, in the middle of the circle. Sounds are sometimes grotesque-high pitched screeching can be explored, deep moaning as well. Resistance and resonance rise from the depths of being. A feeling of the sacred is released in the room, and there is an understanding that the one who experiments in the middle will have to overcome the fear and momentary stagnation that deep encounters with the body evoke. All who witness the student actor's acceptance of this difficult moment know too that the body's impulse is waiting, just underneath the surface, waiting to guide this explorer through to free, emergent movement. This exercise is called Transformations and this is what can happen when the students follow feeling and attend to the primal body.

Young Adulthood: Attending to Nature

The six students, now 22 and participants in a phenomenological research inquiry on the mind–body relationship, wander at the edge of the bluffs overlooking a lake. It is the beginning of the fall season, and they are following feeling as they attend to nature. They wander slowly, breathing, letting go, standing still, being drawn by what catches their eye. They had written about childhood and recent memories in nature, the wonder, the awe, the beauty, the happiness, and gratitude. But the wandering moments are different. These feeling experiments take the group off the beaten track, away from the surety of former experience and into a "present-tense-alive" (Darroch-Lozowski, 2006). They feel the rhythm of the seasons, the senses are awakened, the imagination carries some of them into an act of becoming; a branch, a tree, the stars-feeling carries them into the presence of the cosmos.

The students then gather together in a circle, under the moon. A beautiful energy begins to move through them, gently rocking their bodies, yet their feet feel anchored to the earth. A symbol of interconnectedness appears in their collective experience. Each person's breath floats like mist to the centre of the circle; the feeling of rocking continues. The swaying makes them feel as if they are connected to the core of the earth; some become the vast height of the trees and the vastness of the night sky. These are things that happened when six students, who knew each other for a long time, attended to nature feelingly.

Aostre Johnston (2010) writes that "'Heart' is a metaphor for the deeper dimensions of the human being" (Johnston & Neagley 2011, p. xix). This chapter explores gentling practices that place the student in contact with the deeper dimensions of thought and being. I hope the discussion will contribute to holistic education's aim to allow students the opportunity to feel and to think and to come to experience the role of feeling in the generation of thought. The students who took part in these mind–body experimentations are now in their mid-twenties. They began the drama class when they were between the ages of 7 and 9. Although not a formal representation of research findings (Nigh, 2011), this discussion will feature a few selected insights that have been chosen to show what happens when students follow feeling during mind–body experimentation, both in the drama classroom and in nature. Comments also highlight holistic education's two main pedagogical interests, the mind–body relationship and learning in resonant attunement with the "fundamental realities of nature" (Miller, 2007, p. 3).

Throughout the 12 years that I taught these drama students, warm-up exercises were introduced before every class. A breathing exercise, visualization, yoga, tai chi, energy play, an exercise called Transformations, toning and meditation were all practiced for approximately twenty-minutes prior to the rehearsals. Gradually it became clear that this was not just a period set aside to stretch, warm the muscles, and relax the mind. After certain exercises, the students would share the images they saw in their imaginations and the feeling they experienced in the body. The atmosphere in the room changed. Angela claimed that the atmosphere during these experimentations felt as if it was in an in-between space, thickening and hovering around us. Despite this broadening in our awareness, there was a gentled and focused attentiveness. My curiosity was so captured during these moments that I could not wait to return to these weekly drama classes.

When the students reached adolescence our attitude became more and more experimental. I began to pose questions such as: *What happens when we breathe deeply before the meditation circle? What happens to the energetic sensation throughout the body when we feel emotion?* Through these experiments, I hoped to guide the students into a feeling place within the body, as it seemed that the deeper we travelled into this sensibility, the richer our rehearsals. I also believed that the exercises helped to empty the crowd of thoughts, analysis, and judgment that tend to fill everyday lived experience. However, admittedly I possessed a rather naïve understanding of the relationship between thought and presence in the body (being), often expressing my unexamined belief by telling my students to stop thinking so that we could more easily access feeling. I approach the energetic animation and stillness of being as a function of the feeling state of awareness.

Towards the end of my time with these students, I studied Vivian Dar-roch-Lozowski's (1999, 2006) writing. She claimed that the vegetative region of the body (the feeling centre at the solar plexus) is a place where the mind and body are unified. Our language, thoughts, and actions need to be connected to and informed by this place of unity. The journey to the feeling center began as soon as the student stepped into class and positioned themselves on the floor to quietly breathe. As an actor and singer, I learned through my own experiments with resonance, the imagination, and the body, that there was also a remarkable connection between bodily presence and the free imagination; activating a connection to one seemed to accelerate the other. In graduate school, I also read that Gaston Bachelard (1988) believed, along with William Blake, that the imagination is existence itself and that imagery "is expressive energy" (p. 80). I began to truly wonder if during these classes we were travelling deep into the depths of being, to a place where there was little separation between thought and body.

With the insight that images express existence, I understood a little more about what was occurring in that drama class and why I could feel love in the air. Risk and creative potency were present as we continued to experiment. I was not the only one who could feel this. Isabelle wrote prolifically on the love she felt through the work we did together, and specifically the meditation practice. She described this feeling as a love where each student could become their distinct self as they journeyed together along one path. Bachelard (1988) also wrote that "...love produces images" (p. 20) and images produce love.

Researchers in the field of holistic teaching and learning and mind–body research have focused on the stress-reducing benefits and improvement to learning that certain mind–body practices (e.g., yoga and mindfulness meditation) provide (Miller, 1994; 2007; Murphy, 1992; Kabat-Zin, 2005). Results from studies that compare the stress reducing effects of sports and yoga, for example, show that the calming benefits are sustained far longer and more consistently, after yoga than sports, such as swimming (Berger & Owen, 1988). In this discussion I am talking about a connection to the body that benefits from this sustained calmness, but requires a letting go of goals, intentions, and even skills, so that the student can focus on becoming the internal observer who is aware of their felt sense and open to the imagination.

Participant ideas were expressed through journal writing, interviews, conversations at cafes, and talks while sitting by the lake. During the first phase of the research, Isabelle, Angela, Gwendolyn, Rose, Dylan, and Digby were asked to describe what it was like to explore the mind–body relationship in the drama classroom as they were growing up. During the second phase the students agreed to explore the mind–body dynamic in nature;

the intention was to take up the following question as a group inquiry: *What happens when we attend to nature feelingly?* (Darroch-Lozowski, 2006). I also wanted to experientially investigate Miller's (2008) statement: "Holistic education attempts to bring education into alignment with the fundamental realities of nature" (p. 3). Before starting the research, I believed that our mind–body experimentations placed us in a vulnerable, open, and sensitive space, one in which an alignment with nature might be possible. I thought that if we simply looked into nature with the sensitivity and calmness that the mind–body exploration offered, perhaps we might learn something new about the relationship between the fundamental realities of nature and learning.

GENTLING PRACTICES AND STUDENT INSIGHTS

Get out of your head and get into your heart. Think less, feel more.
—Osho

Vivian Darroch-Lozowski (2006) has written that while emotion leads to the awareness of the separation between self and other, feeling harmonizes or resonates with what is occurring in the present. Affirming the view that feeling is a unique state of awareness, Antonio Damasio (1994, 1999) claims that feeling facilitates a distinct form of internal witness. During the feeling state of consciousness, the individual attends to both what is happening in the body and to that which is occurring with the self as thoughts flow by.

Breathing

Attending to the flow and feeling of the breath is the foundation and beginning point for all mind–body practices. The drama students began the class quietly breathing as they lay on the floor, their hands placed on the solar plexus. No effort to control or manipulate the breath is necessary; breathing without judgement fosters an alignment with the feeling center. Isabelle, Rose, and Angela acknowledged the overall calming, gentling, and focusing effects of the breathing exercise. As a grade six student, Angela remembered a visitor that came to her school to teach the students about breathing. She was surprised that a lot of her classmates did not know that the stomach rises during the inhalation and falls during the exhalation. Rose also reported that while acting on stage, authentic emotion is more easily accessed through awareness to the breath.

The Meditation Circle

Transpersonal psychologist Carl Jung (1965) believed that images, when meaningfully explored, hold an important key to the individuation process. Jung also believed that feeling was responsible for generating the awareness of imagery. The meditation provided the students the opportunity to encounter their images, and it was one of the most intriguing activities I have experienced as a teacher. Sometimes it is easy to think that the imagination takes us away from reality. Bachelard (1988) undermines this notion: "To imagine, then, is to heighten the tone of reality" (p. 81). Perhaps Jung and my students would say that the imagination deepens the tone of reality. No matter. What is clear is that the imagination is necessary for a more nuanced understanding of lived experience. For three minutes it felt as if the class was immersed in an ocean that was for one moment still and another moment swirling and eddying around the circle. The students' bodies were relaxed; their hands tingled and their faces were filled with fascination. While listening to resonances between the students' meditation experiences, I began to witness how feeling and the imagination foster the interconnectedness of human consciousness. When we travel to the depths of our being together, we are both distinctly alone and connected to others' thoughts and feelings.

During the research inquiry, Gwen and Dylan addressed the interconnectedness of the meditation circle when they recalled how surprised they were that students would continually see the same image or think the same thought as someone else had in the circle. Gwen even wondered if we were catching pieces of one another. Bachelard (1988) sheds light on this phenomenon: "If the *imagination* is really the power that forms human thoughts, we can easily understand that the transmission of thoughts can only take place between two imaginations that are already in accord" (p. 120).

Isabelle's journal describes the influence that the meditation practice had on her personal development and learning:

> The group nurtured an environment of openness to new experience like none I have ever encountered . . . I think it is trying to discover what it is that I now understand but has taken me 10 years to understand. This project is seeking to understand the new way of being and of learning and of seeing the world that I came to know through the work we did as a group . . . But I digress. Through these meditations I have come to know myself better . . . Each image I saw (and still see) was a part of me and my life being reflected back for me to see. It was as if I was allowed to have a look at what Isabelle was struggling with, what Isabelle was excited about . . . (Isabelle)

Isabelle claimed that the exploratory nature of our work allowed her to let go of the linear or goal-oriented ways in which she usually lived her life. Ironically, however, she identifies what I believe to be a viable and profound evolutionary sequence in her being-learning-seeing statement.

Transformations

The gentling activities that I have described thus far require an acceptance of what is, an awareness of felt sense, an attention to the flow of thought and a fluid and free imagination. With the Transformations exercise, the imagination and thought do not disappear, but function in complete alignment with the body's impulses; thought and the imagination are attuned with the body, meaning they live in the stretch of a hand and the pressing of the foot into the ground. The exercise carries the student into a sometimes terrifying unknown, as the class empathetically holds the space for the person who is experimenting in the middle of the circle.

Existing within the primal body allows the student to attune to their instincts viscerally and to become aware of the typically ignored or rejected parts of the body. During mid-adolescence, the students were old enough and established in their relationships with each other that they could enter into the exercise with the respect necessary for a process that relied on both vulnerability and courage. During the research inquiry, the students were asked to describe what it was like to shift from focusing on their thoughts to focusing on their capacity to follow deep feeling. Rose explained her understanding:

> I can remember witnessing it . . . You can tell when-like you can tell the transition occurs but I don't know what that point looks like...its like connected to the visual but its not so visual, its instinctive but its sort of energy- connection-like group dynamic I guess or like the amount of concentration you are putting into their work. You have to have that, that whole faith and witness it. (Rose)

The students' capacity to shift from identifying with their thoughts to following feeling was enhanced by remaining within themselves, developing a sense of "whole faith" and becoming a witness that does not primarily rely on seeing as we typically use this sense to navigate our material lives.

Digby also explained that becoming overly analytical has serious ontological implications. During the Transformations exercise, he realized that he was more open. More importantly, "You are out of character when you start to overanalyze every little nuance that you are doing." Dylan came to different conclusions, but shared the feeling that she was giving up her identification with thought by surrendering to the body. During the nature phase of the inquiry, Dylan described a feeling of surrender after we explored the

Transformations exercise outside: ". . . you are not actually moving yourself and you are not actually making any sounds; something else is doing it for you and you get to watch." Directly after the exercise, Dylan quietly wandered in nature: "I looked out at the water and for once felt nothing, I saw nothing. I thought of nothing, and, for once, it was nice. I've never really been able to turn off the volume on my mind but the lake's ripples pressed the mute button. I didn't even try." "I didn't even try" reveals that the will surrenders, both during a fundamental connection to the body and during moments of concentrated attention in nature.

As holistic educators, we should understand that the deeper waters of human consciousness are aligned with the elemental movements of nature, such as disappearing and reappearing, filling and emptying, rising and falling; authentic learning derives from a tacit engagement with these natural movements. To truly align with the fundamental realities of nature our personal goals and agendas must be set aside. Emptying, disappearing, and falling can be terrifying when you are accustomed to thinking that learning is about constantly accruing knowledge and that thinking occurs only within the subjective closed self.

TRANSFORMATION:
THE FUNDAMENTAL REALITY OF NATURE

I wonder if we as educators take the time to really question if our students understand the nature of their own thoughts or consciousness. How we relate to thought, its pattern and movement, should be approached as a mystery well worth pursuing. Many emergent thoughts, hidden within the deep presence of our being, remain hidden and under accessed, as these thoughts have not yet found a way to rise to awareness. Thought should be aligned with nature and the body's way of knowing so that its development remains connected to natural processes. Through dreams, our movements and attending, emergent thought awaits the open witness who possesses a "whole faith." Bachelard (1988) claimed that during certain encounters with being, there is a cessation of language and sight: "The most profound dream is essentially a phenomenon of visual and verbal *repose*" (p. 26).

Vivian Darroch-Lozowski (1999) refers to thought as our ongoingness, and if this is so, a connection to nature is the most powerful context in which to witness thought. As we struggle collectively across the globe with the shadow of human life on earth, our tendencies towards fundamentalist thinking, our war-like ontology, and the earth's climate challenges, would it not benefit us to return to the beginning, slow down, and empty our minds of what we should or should not do and surrender to the fundamental reality of existence itself?

On the evening that the group experienced a transformation in nature our expectations were soft and simple. We just wanted to stand in silence together and meditate, like we used to. After we were outside under the moon for a few moments, a distinct rocking sensation slowly moved through us. The more intense the rocking, the more a feeling of being anchored to the earth's core was present. The imagination played its part. Gwen felt a lengthening through the spine as she "became" the tree she gazed on. Angela felt herself shoot upwards into the stars. Dylan and Rose saw their breath turn to warm fog and stream into the middle of the circle. Although Digby said that he could not reach a meditative state, as his five female friends did, his remarkable language capabilities were revealed when he translated his friends' experiences into metaphors. He claimed that the whole experience was "forming a maelstrom." Indeed, it felt like that, energy streaming around a circle, flowing into the centre, inwards, flying upwards and yet creating a downward pull. Bachelard (1988) beautifully acknowledged a confluence between energy and the imagination: "For Blake, dynamic imagination is an inquiry into energy" (p. 81).

The participants' transcribed statements showed that something occurred that evening that powerfully activated the imagination and feeling. Noting rationality's repose during this experience, I imagine that Bachelard (1988) might suggest that our group had fallen momentarily into nature's dream. All of these statements, however, are simply wonderings and conjecture. What I do know is that this experience occurred because together we had formed a habit of following deep feeling, observing the imagination, and bearing witness to thought. And on that night, our gentling habits, the simple practices of our desire for collective receptivity and openness, placed the group in the path of one of nature's fundamental realities, the unexpected.

REFERENCES

Bachelard, G. (1943/1988). *Air and dreams: An essay of the imagination of movement.* Texas: Dallas Institute Publications.

Berger, B., & Owen, D. (1988). Stress reduction and mood enhancement in four exercise modes: Swimming, body conditioning, hatha yoga, and fencing. *Research Quarterly for Exercise and Sport, 59*(2), 148–159.

Damasio, A. R. (1999). *The feeling of what happens: Body and emotion in the making of consciousness.* New York: Harcourt Brace.

Damasio, A. R. (1994). *Descartes' error: Emotion, reason, and the human brain.* New York, NY: Putnam's Sons.

Darroch-Lozowski, V. (2006). Re-patterning global warming. *Environmentalist.* (26), 195–200.

Darroch-Lozowski. V. (1999). *The uncoded world: A poetic semiosis of the wandered.* New York, NY: Peter Lang.

Johnston, A., & Webb Neagley, M. (Eds.). (2011). *Educating from the Heart: Theoretical and practical approaches to transforming education.* Maryland: Rowan and Littlefield Education.

Jung, C. G. (1965). *Memories, dreams, reflections.* New York, NY: Random House.

Kabat-Zin, J. (2005). *Coming to our senses: Healing ourselves through mindfulness.* New York, NY: Hyperion.

Miller, J. P. (1994). *The contemplative practitioner: Meditation in education and the professions.* Westport, CT: Bergin and Garvey.

Miller, J. P. (2008). *The holistic curriculum.* Toronto: University of Toronto Press.

Nigh, K. (2011). *Holistic education: The flow and pulse of learning.* (Unpublished doctoral dissertation). University of Toronto, Toronto, Ontario.

Murphy, M. (1992). *The future of the body: Explorations into the further evolution of human nature.* New York, NY: Putnam.

CHAPTER 17

THE PRESENCE OF THE THINKING HEART IN THE LANGUAGE TEACHING–LEARNING RELATIONSHIP

Merlin Charles
University of Toronto

INTRODUCTION: DISCOVERING THE HEART TO TEACH

I have always been passionate about language teaching and learning and having the opportunity to follow my heart and to actually become a language teacher has been like a dream come true. As I reflect on my teaching practice and what it means to teach from the heart, I feel compelled to acknowledge the land of my birth and where it all began. There is no doubt that my learning experiences in Dominica—also known as the nature island of the Caribbean—became the catalyst for my keen interest in languages and holistic education. As Lewis (2007) ponders:

> What happens to a people surrounded by beauty and infused with wonder? How does our environment—the soil we set our roots down in, the sun and

Teaching From the Thinking Heart, pages 149–157
Copyright © 2014 by Information Age Publishing
All rights of reproduction in any form reserved.

space we share, the water we wet our souls with—affect the slow growth of our own spirits and the shape they will finally take? For both, instructor and students, the answers to these questions—the responses of our spirits—come in surprising and significant ways. (p. 99)

In retrospect, I find much resonance with this statement as I can still vividly recall the awe and wonder of the natural beauty which enveloped me as we joyfully sang songs and recited poetry underneath the trees outside our one-room school house. Memories of the lush green vegetation, the gentle whisper of the wind, the warm glow of the Caribbean sun are still vivid in my imagination as I prepare my lessons. In addition, the vibrant linguistic environment in which I grew up also provided a rich and fascinating arena for helping me discover my love for language and its impact on social interaction. While negotiating my identity among the three languages—Creole, English, and French—I find resonance with Cook's affirmation that: "Language is the centre of human life . . . through language we plan our lives and remember our past; we exchange ideas and experiences; we form our social and individual identities" (2001, p. 1).

With regards to my teacher identity, the following quote from Palmer (1998) aptly captures the essence of my experience when he says that:

Many of us were called to teach by encountering not only a mentor but also a particular field of study. We were drawn to a body of knowledge because it shed light on our identity as well as on the world. We did not merely find a subject to teach—the subject also found us. We may recover the heart to teach by remembering how that subject evoked a sense of self that was only dormant in us before we encountered the subject's way of naming and framing life. (p. 26)

Indeed, I can safely say that not only was I drawn to the French language, I believe that the language also found me, and certainly evoked in me "the heart to teach." Over the years, this heart to teach has also been nurtured by the many mentors whom I have encountered throughout my "apprenticeship of observation"[1] as a language learner in various contexts: The patience and kindness of my high school French teacher in Dominica, the creativity and resourcefulness of my postsecondary professors in both France and Canada have had a significant impact on my journey as an educator. Moreover, in this chapter, I will integrate various insights gained from my doctoral work, my on-going research on teaching presence along with regular dialogue with colleagues and students; these have been a constant source of inspiration as I continue to reflect on my own practice of heart in teaching.

My first "real" teaching opportunity presented itself when I began my MA program in French Language and Literature at the Department of French

Studies, University of Toronto. As this teaching assignment involved helping students develop their listening skills and oral proficiency, it became a real joy to share my tremendous love of the language with others and to inspire them to do the same. During our one-hour weekly tutorials, I found it was quite easy to connect with the 15–20 students who were enrolled in my classes. I tried to make my lessons fun and interesting; I would tell them stories about my own journey as a second language learner, and help them gain an appreciation of the various francophone cultures through poetry and song. I was encouraged by the responsiveness of the students and their positive feedback regarding this approach.

REFLECTIONS AND QUESTIONS FROM THE HEART

However, as my responsibilities "evolved" and I became a college professor and a "sole responsibility" university instructor, things began to change. Not only had the class size increased, I had the tendency—as was expected—to focus too heavily on the course descriptions, and the question of "how"—in other words, the methods. How am I going to proceed? How am I going explain the objectives of the course to students? How are they going to be evaluated? I soon realized that this was in fact a prescription, which really does not allow much room for actually getting to know students and identifying their needs. I noticed that in my classes, there were students who were very strong in one of the areas of language but weak in others, so it became increasingly important to develop an awareness of students' strengths and their weaknesses. I pondered the idea of how great it would be to write the course description after having met the students and identifying their needs and what they really want to achieve. But alas, this approach did not quite fit into the design of university programs and courses. And besides, as one of my colleagues cautioned, some students prefer to sit on the sidelines: "Some students think of university studies as sitting in a lecture hall and taking notes and listening, and you know, being enlightened about a subject."

Being faced with these challenges, I began to ask myself some new questions—the "what if" questions. What if they don't like me or my teaching style? What if I am not able to deliver? What if I get a poor evaluation from students? As I contemplated these questions, the answer seemed to be embedded in yet another overarching question: how do I adapt a style of teaching which would allow me to connect with my students, identify and attend to their needs, and be present to them? In other words, how do I reclaim the "heart of teaching" in the postsecondary French Language Learning (FLL) context?

MODELLING THE THINKING HEART

In my quest to answer these questions, and as I gained more experience in my teaching practice, while simultaneously pursuing my doctoral studies in holistic approaches to language teaching-learning, I became increasingly aware of the importance of practicing the thinking heart. Based on my doctoral work (Charles, 2012) and my on-going research on teaching presence, I developed a model (see Figure 17.1), which was designed to help me in this endeavor.

As depicted in the model, the symbol of the heart is prominently featured at the centre, given its important role in "operationalizing" the process of teaching. Surrounding the heart are other words and images which all contribute, in varying degrees, to the practice of the thinking heart. To give a brief overview: the hands represent the three R's—responsibility, respect, and relationship; the U represents the word "university" as well as the Theory of the U^2 (Senge et al., 2005); the arrows represent the idea of "flow" (Csikszentmihalyi, 1990) and interdependence (Johnson & Johnson, 1994). The concentric circles which intersect the heart represent the 3Ts—Transmission, Transaction, and Transformation (Miller & Seller, 1990); it is important to note that the word "transformation" is depicted in the heart itself. The words "open heart/open mind/open will" represent Rachel Kessler's (2000) notion of "teaching presence" which, in turn overarches the model. Last but not least, there is the word "love," which, of course, is at the heart of teaching. An understanding of the relationship between the concepts in this integrated framework has helped to redefine

Figure 17.1 The heart and soul of language teaching: an integrated framework

my orientation to curriculum and to better adopt the practices of the thinking heart in my current teaching context. In the following section, I will share some of these practices by drawing on concepts from the model, interspersed with comments/feedback received from research participants as well as colleagues and students.

RECLAIMING THE HEART TO TEACH

What I have learned from my research as well as my on-going practice in the language classroom is that teaching presence is fundamental to effective learning and is directly connected to the thinking heart. As I prepare for every new semester, I constantly remind myself, not only of my role and responsibilities, but I also try to find purpose in what I do. My goal, therefore, is to make a conscious effort to be present to my students—both physically and emotionally; to be authentic, friendly, and approachable; to be aware of their needs and accepting of their humanness; to foster positive communication, respectful discipline, and trust. I recognize therefore that ultimately, I need to get to know my students and ensure that everyone has a holistic, fulfilling learning experience. But I also realize that in order to be present to my students, I need to "cultivate" my own presence.

While preparing for the beginning of every new class, I try to be present to myself: I try to connect with my inner self by engaging in deep breathing and a loving-kindness' meditation;[3] I take frequent breaks in between my lesson planning to go for a walk, listen to a song, or even watch pictures of Dominica; I visualize the joy of "being there" with the students, their eagerness to learn and grow, and the common goal that we all share. To borrow the words of Sitelle, one of my research participants, "We're all in this boat together!" So instead of overly stressing the objectives, or creating undue anxiety about the outcomes and evaluations of the course, I have become more inclined to put my energy into the initial precious moments together, to truly bond with my students. As Miller (2007) asserts, "The focus of holistic education is on relationships" (p. 13). Similarly, Cummins (2001) places relationships "at the heart of teaching" (p. 1).

I bear this in mind as I begin each class, and I try to get to know my students well, without infringing on their personal space. The beginning of every semester, or my first encounter with students, has become the most exciting/important moment for me (and hopefully for them). I encourage students to talk about their interests, about what they are studying, and their various backgrounds. I do this systematically, by making a concerted effort to get to know them all. I try to learn the names of my students by the end of the first week. To me, that's very important, because that's the first bond that I establish. In addition to showing enthusiasm, I invite each student to introduce him/herself and I try to establish eye contact with everybody. I greet each student with a warm, friendly smile as I acknowledge their presence and welcome them to the class. It becomes an opportunity for students to get to know me, and to get to know each other. Given that language classes—even at the postsecondary level—are generally small (fewer than 30 students), I have developed quite a few techniques, which have helped me to learn my students' names.

In order to facilitate this process in large lecture halls with sometimes 70 students (which is the most I have had in one class), I would bring along markers/crayons and provide blank (8 x 11) sheets of paper and invite them to write and display their names on their desks. From this initial "assignment," I get a glimpse of students' personalities/sense of style by the creative ways in which they write their names. At the end of the class, I would then collect the names, and in the subsequent class, I would call each student by name as I hand over his or her name tag. I find this a great way of fostering a spirit of connectedness and inclusiveness in the classroom; it also serves as neat way of keeping attendance.

As the semester progresses, I design my lessons in such a way as to integrate questions that allow me to get to know students. Apart from having frequent chats with them, I try to become more accessible to students by opening up various lines of communication. I encourage them to drop by during my office hours, to make an appointment to come talk to me, or to contact me through email. To me, this open door policy ties in with the whole idea of having an "open will." Moreover, this has also proven to be quite helpful, because not only do I get to develop a bond with my students, it is also an opportunity to provide clarification on certain issues, to get their feedback on my teaching, and to allow me to continually assist in transforming their learning experience. Synonymous with what Maigret, one of my research participants so aptly describes as "verbal warmth," these are some of the ways in which I try to "be there" for my students and to establish and maintain good relationships with them. I have continued to have an open heart in my classes due to the positive feedback that I receive from my students, as evidenced by the following comment which I find quite endearing: "Merlin . . . cares so much about her students! . . . Her lectures are great because she doesn't talk *to* you, she talks *with* you . . . "

In my classes, I try to offer a variety of activities (including games, debates, role play, skits), which are designed to actively engage students as well as facilitate "flow" and participation. I have come to realize that what may appear as passivity in some students, may in fact be fear or anxiety about participating because they do not want to feel humiliated if they have not performed appropriately. This is particularly true for second language learners. Yannick—one of the core participants in my study—helped shed some light on this dilemma as follows: "When you speak a language it's really yourself that you're putting at risk and it's a lot more threatening to be actually saying something in French in front of your peers or your teacher than it is to write a [mathematical] formula on the board. . . ." This insight raised my awareness that my presence as a language instructor should help students feel comfortable in the classroom and transform students who appear to be passive into active participants. Using the 3Ts as a pedagogical tool, I try to go beyond the mere transmission of knowledge and orient my teaching towards transformation by integrating a variety of methods, strategies, and techniques that place emphasis on the more active skills.

I have found that another way of facilitating flow in my classroom is by ensuring that students feel good about participating. I therefore try to reward students with compliments. Even though there are times when students offer answers that are not quite correct, I try to be gentle, patient, and kind, by giving them ample time to reformulate their answers. According to one of my participants, "It's empathy, I think, it's sensitivity. It's not always present at university." In the many activities which require teamwork, I ensure that group members are supportive of and sensitive to each other's needs, thereby encouraging cooperation instead of competition.

One of the most important ways that I have learned to cultivate and maintain my teaching presence in the classroom is by sharing with my students who I am, what I am passionate about, and inviting them to do the same. This pedagogical openness was affirmed by Patrice, a postsecondary FL teacher, who shared that:

> Before I can know who my student is, I need to know who I am. I need to know what is important to me, what my values are, what my beliefs are, and I need to bring that into the classroom with me, not in a fundamentalist way.

This is something that I struggled with in my practice. When I first started teaching, there was this nagging reminder of the words of a well-meaning colleague who offered the following advice: "Make sure you get your students to respect you. Don't smile too much or joke around with them!" For months, I felt paralyzed by this thought! What made this even more daunting was that this idea of "not smiling 'til Christmas" in order to gain and maintain students' respect, also appeared in some of the literature that I read. *Of course every teacher deserves to be respected; in fact, teaching presence calls for respectful discipline.* But I couldn't quite fathom the idea that there was a risk of losing students' respect if I reveal to them the sheer joy that I feel in my heart, by just being in the classroom with them, sharing my *joie de vivre* through laughter, jokes, music, dance, or other expressions of language and culture. It was quite a relief to know that, as Maigret affirms, "You can't teach a language effectively—well, maybe I shouldn't say that, I'll say it anyway—by being overly serious, and overly judgmental." More importantly, based on feedback from students, it is clear that being cheerful and having a sense of humor really helps to make the class "light-hearted" while at the same time enhancing their learning experience.

So, I have reclaimed my heart to teach by being and sharing who I am with my students. One of these, for example, is my love for music. To begin each course, I introduce an *exercice de rechauffement* (or a warm up exercise). I would first model this activity by playing one of my favorite songs (in French), explain its particular social/cultural context, show the YouTube version (if available), and encourage students to share their thoughts and feelings. I then invite an enthusiastic volunteer to share a song for the following class, and this becomes a regular feature throughout the semester. The benefits of this *exercice de rechauffement* are threefold: it helps to start off the class on a light and happy note; it celebrates cultural diversity; and it gives students the opportunity to contribute and participate actively in the class.

Alternately, I would also integrate what I call a *partage* (sharing) where students are encouraged to share their interests with the rest of the class—a short poem, an artefact, a video, etc., relating to other aspects of French language and culture. Students also learn to take responsibility for their own learning, while applying their language skills. Through the process of engaging in this activity—surfing the net in French, or talking to francophones—students learn to develop linguistic and communication skills while at the same time discovering an element of self-knowledge. We generally enjoy these heart-warming moments of interaction; it is an opportunity for students to feel good about themselves and to celebrate each other's talents. Though simple, these "soulful learning" activities really touch the heart, because they help students construct knowledge about the language/culture and foster positive relationships in their classrooms, on campus, and in the wider francophone community.

This spirit of positive interdependence, to me, relates to Martin Luther King's concept of a beloved community and, essentially, the notion of Ubuntu, which Mandela (1997) describes as a process of embracing our own humanity and that of other human beings in our quest for a better world. As I cultivate my teaching presence, I consciously try to create this beloved community in my classroom, by nurturing positive relationships, fostering respect for individual and community consciousness, a full acceptance of each other, and, most importantly, love.

NOTES

1. Darling-Hammond (2006) describes this concept as "the learning that takes place by virtue of being a student for twelve or more years in traditional classroom settings" (p. 35).

2. Also referred to as "Theory U" (see Sharmar (2007), this explores the notion of presence as a natural, whole, and interconnected process.
3. A practice that I was first introduced to in Jack Miller's course entitled "The Holistic Curriculum."

REFERENCES

Charles, M. (2012). *The heart and soul of language teaching: Making interconnections between holistic and second language education in the post-secondary context.* (Doctoral Dissertation). Retrieved from https://tspace.library.utoronto.ca/bitstream/1807/32680/3/Charles_Merlin_201206_PhD_thesis.pdf

Cook, V. (2001). *Second language learning and teaching.* (3rd Ed.) London: Arnold Publishers.

Cummins, J. (2001). *Negotiating identities: Education for empowerment in a diverse society.* (2nd ed.) Los Angeles: California Association for Bilingual Education

Csikszentmihalyi, M. (1990). *Flow: The psychology of optimal experience.* New York: HarperCollins.

Johnson, R. T., & Johnson, D. W. (1994). An overview of cooperative learning. In J. Thousand, A. Villa, & A. Nevin (Eds.), *Creativity and collaborative learning* (pp. 1–23). Baltimore: Brookes Press.

Kessler, R. (2000). The teaching presence. *Virginia Journal of Education, 944*(2), 7–10.

Lewis, C. (2007). Spirit rooted in place: Field studies in pedagogical paradigm for creating change. In S. Shelton-Colangelo, C. Mancuso, & M. Duvall (Eds.), *Teaching with joy: Educational practices for the twenty-first century.* Lanham, Maryland: Rowman and Littlefield Publishers, Inc.

Mandela, N. (1997, July 11). *Renewal and renaissance—Towards a new world order.* Lecture by President Nelson Mandela at the Oxford Centre for Islamic Studies, Oxford, UK.

Miller, J. P. (2007). *The holistic curriculum.* Toronto: University of Toronto Press.

Miller J. P., & Seller W. (1985/1990). *Curriculum: Perspectives and practice.* New York: Longman.

Palmer, P. (1998). *The courage to teach: Exploring the inner landscape of a teacher's life.* San Francisco, C.A: Jossey-Bass.

Senge, P., Scharmer, C., Jaworski, J., & Flowers, B. (2005). *Presence: An exploration of profound change in people, organizations, and society.* New York: Doubleday.

SECTION III

NARRATIVES

CHAPTER 18

SOLITUDE IN TEACHING

Jill Morris
University of Toronto

"Best Society," a poem by Philip Larkin, is quoted in *Solitude and Loneliness: a Buddhist View,* by Sarvananda (Alastair Jessiman). The poem in its entirety speaks to me in its telling of the gradual shift from a childhood ubiquity of solitude and an unquestioned completeness of the child-self to a socially mandated re-orientation outward to define the self in terms of the other. In defining ourselves in terms of our relations to others, the performance of self becomes the acceptable form and the unconditioned self that lies in solitude is marked as the "compensating make-believe." In the final stanza, the poetic voice strikes an angry retreat:

> Viciously, then, I lock my door.
> The gas-fire breathes. The wind outside
> Ushers in evening rain. Once more
> Uncontradicting solitude
> Supports me on its giant palm;
> And like a sea-anemone
> Or simple snail, there cautiously
> Unfolds, emerges, what I am.

Teaching From the Thinking Heart, pages 161–170
Copyright © 2014 by Information Age Publishing

While the energy of that anger is familiar to me, I resonate especially with the line, "Uncontradicting solitude." My own body vibrates with the feeling of peace that comes over me when I am able, finally, to close the door and feel whole, to be done with the contradictions of navigating the world. I am able to be all myself, and at once I am not measuring this self or that. I feel no lack or absence, and, like solitude itself, I am "A plentiful and obvious thing/Not at all hard to understand." I am drawn to Larkin's choice of images for the unfolding of the self in this recovered solitude: an anemone is delicate and beautiful only in its element, only as it is left alone. It is not a mighty animal, hardly much beyond the poem's other image of the snail. This self I find in solitude is not and does not need to be grand or epic; the self that I claim in solitude is not ego driven. In this paper I have set for myself the task of exploring my experiences, both personally and professionally, with claiming solitude without apology and considering the strengths and benefits of solitude in teaching and learning.

PERSONAL CONTEXT

Solitude has long been a part of my life but I have only recently begun to embrace it. Currently, I regularly seek out opportunities to be alone. When I am in crowds, I look for a situation that allows me the most distance from others or a feeling of greater isolation. I will sit in an area that is removed from most people. I will arrange my position so that I am looking out over an open space with my back to the crowd. I feel that I need that space. When I am unable to achieve that distance—either physically or as a perception—then it can take some time for me to settle in and be comfortable in a group situation. I avoid parties, festivals, and congested walkways. At earlier points in my life, I don't remember being quite so exacting about the comfort I tried to achieve in increasing degrees of aloneness, but I would say that I liked being alone. I was a "reader" and would prefer hours alone reading to most group activities. Then, reading was a more common activity for children, and in my household reading was valued highly; my father, being an academic, modeled a particular type of solitary activity that was socially acceptable because it involved reading and writing. I was encouraged to read, and I think I likely saw it as a good way to be alone with parental support. My identity as an academic probably stems, in part, from this. Even now, I use my work as a reason to be alone; my partner is much more gregarious than I am and would be happier in my company but he respects the quiet, private space that is afforded to academic work. I can be alone without any social consequences, and the relief that comes from this is significant because it makes clear that I continue to be sensitive to judgment with regards to my desire for solitude. As a child—or even looking back and making sense of my childhood—I tended to think of my preference for solitary time in a socially negative manner, primarily because that is the way in which society constructed and still constructs what I would now name my tendency to introversion. I did not have private shame about my desire for solitude, but I understood it as antisocial. This is, more or less, still the case.

I could force myself to be very adept at social interaction. I went through a significant phase in my young adult life in which I was actually the "life of the party." For years I served as the social hub for a good size group of friends. But this was made possible by alcohol and other mood-altering substances, and it was not a sustainable or positive expression of self. I remember coming to the conclusion that I did not want to continue to put energy into this way of being anymore. It feels significant that I actually had to "confess" this. I also remember the fear I felt at what this would mean for me. I felt certain that I would no longer have a place in the world, and that my friends would not be there if I could not perform for them. To some extent my fears were justified; the world is better suited to an extrovert expression, and I did lose friends. But I gained in energy because I was no longer expending so much on projecting this pretend self, and I gained in time because I no longer had to attend to the parties of the world. Eventually, I found I had friends that understood and appreciated my way of being.

PROFESSIONAL CONTEXT

As I think about my presence in the classroom now, I find it difficult to remember a time when speaking in front of a group of people was difficult. I am certain that the students and teachers I work with would be surprised to hear that I consider my personality as primarily introverted. I accept the responsibility of "social hub" in my classroom; I am reasonably confident that most people I work with would say I have a marked dynamic in the classroom and the school community. I work hard to model thoughtful and confident expression of ideas and questions; I make a subject of myself so that others need not, and this has always felt important to me as a teacher committed to the relative emotional safety of my students. As I describe this, it is becoming clear that I am able to perform an extroverted role because it is necessary—it is not an expression of what I feel is my authentic self; rather, it is a technique or strategy I use in my teaching. In my earliest days of teaching, I would say that I prided myself on the force of my personality in the classroom. My underlying comfort with introversion and my work with antioppression educational theory and political literary theory helped me to develop and maintain a critique of the implications of the "force of my personality." I still think that a degree of extroversion is important in a teacher, but my reflective practice, my study of Buddhist philosophy, and my growing acceptance of my authentic and likely introverted self has opened up new possibilities for my "presence" in the classroom.

My early years of teaching were whirlwinds of activity and, mostly, joyful uncertainty. I worried and planned and reworked as I juggled new skills and responsibilities. There was less time for solitude—and probably greater need for it. I could liken my earliest years to the work of an untrained singer: I had the passion for singing but I wasn't bringing it into my diaphragm. Consequently, I was straining my voice. I made myself hit most of those notes by sheer force of will but, for the most part, it wasn't coming from the belly. I have a clear memory of a span of time in which I had been up late planning lessons and rising early to go in to school and set up activities, days full of teaching and meeting with students and colleagues. On a final Friday afternoon I called a taxi to carry me home because I didn't have the physical or emotional energy to negotiate the local transit. I sat in the back seat with my arms limp at my side and wept quietly. I wasn't sad; I was utterly depleted. Clearly, this was not sustainable for anyone, but as someone who reaped so much replenishment from solitude, it was especially draining. I loved teaching—planning was creative and satisfying, I didn't resent staying up to 2:00 a.m. finding resources and coming up with engaging approaches to challenging and relevant ideas. I was joyfully engaged in the non-hierarchical administrative structure of my school community; I was excited by my connections with students and parents. I knew I was in a wonderful situation in which I was both supported and challenged. And yet, despite so many indisputably positive elements in my life, I was experiencing very dark times of frightening self-doubt. At this time, I found my way to meditation and although it was in direct response to a personal crisis, it was equally true that I was driven by a desire to do service to my role as an educator. It was through meditation that I managed to reassert time and space for solitude in my life. It seems counter-intuitive that what could be construed as withdrawal was the key to my return to an authentic and sustainable engagement with my life and work, but that was doubtless the case.

To be sure, there are many other important realizations that came from meditation but while my meditation practice has been inconsistent over the ensuing years, solitude has remained a constant positive aspect in my personal and professional equilibrium. Meditation heightens my appreciation of a conscious fostering of nourishing solitude. Reflecting on the role it has played in my teaching practice has allowed me to appreciate how my teaching has deepened through my experiences and the awareness I have found: I still work to encourage confident, critical, and thoughtful engagement with ideas but I believe I am becoming less performative in this and more *present.* When I ensure the physical, emotional, and spiritual space, "Uncontradicting solitude/Supports me on its giant palm," and I am able to "unfold," "emerge," to be "what I am," and this is the wholehearted example I wish to set for my students.

QUESTIONING SOLITUDE

The connection between solitude and my ability to be wholehearted in my classroom was an important personal realization; it had a direct positive effect on my teaching and, I believe, on student learning, but, as Larkin's poem reminds us, solitude is something that continues to be suspect in our society. This mistrust or devaluing of solitude reveals itself in most aspects of our school system from bureaucratic structures to curriculum expectations and teaching strategies. I wanted to learn and think more about the cultural and historical context for our perspectives on solitude. To do this, I read the currently popular book *Quiet: The Power of Introverts in a World that Can't Stop Talking* by Susan Cain (2013).

It never fails to surprise me how easily people, myself included, assume that our current cultural attitudes and actions are timeless and absolute. Exposure to the history of cultural norms can go a long way towards loosening the hold of unproductive or destructive habits of mind. In her book, Cain introduces a persuasive argument regarding American culture that suggests a simple shift from what "cultural historian Warren Susman called a Culture of Character to a Culture of Personality" (Cain, 2013, p. 21). According to Cain's interpretation of Susman's theory, "[i]n the Culture of Character, the ideal self was serious, disciplined, and honorable. What counted was not so much the impression one made in public as how one behaved in private." In contrast, "when they embraced the Culture of Personality, Americans started to focus on how others perceived them" (p. 21).

The obvious connection to Larkin's poem suggests that this shift was reasonably not just an American phenomenon. Susman's argument is that with the rise of the Industrial Age came a shift in thinking that prioritized the outward performance of the individual over private, core values. As people moved increasingly to city centers, they had more exposure to others but fewer authentic connections with the people around them. In a rural setting, you could be known by your character because people shared histories with one another, had seen the actions of their neighbors over time. In the anonymous city, where people were now competing for industrial based jobs, "'citizens' morphed into 'employees'" (Cain, 2013 p. 22). Quiet strengths, reserve, modesty, and humility were effectively invisible in a society that was increasingly dependent on competitive first impressions. Inward focused self-improvement texts such as *The Pilgrim's Progress* or the essays of Emerson were replaced by the now classic book by Dale Carnegie, *How to Win Friends and Influence People.* Psychology introduced the inferiority complex, responding and contributing to the growing social stigma towards reserved personalities by pathologizing characteristics that were not aggressively confident (p. 26). If you were not "out there" you were not doing it right. This would, of course, have implications for parenting and schools. As Cain notes:

> Well-meaning parents of the midcentury agreed that quiet was unacceptable and gregariousness ideal for both girls and boys. Some discouraged their children from solitary and serious hobbies, like classical music, that could make them unpopular. They sent their kids to school at increasingly young ages, where the main assignment was learning to socialize. Introverted children were often singled out as problem cases. (p. 27)

The rise in the Culture of Personality was matched by Hollywood culture and advertising media. Ultimately, the insecurity and competition inherent in this new thrust would become normalized. Pharmaceutical companies capitalized on this and "...in 1955 a drug company named Carter-Wallace released the antianxiety drug Miltown, reframing anxiety as the natural product of a society that was both dog-eat-dog and relentlessly social" (p. 29). While the "man of action" was not invented in mid-twentieth-century America, the speed of the modern industrial age not only made it increasingly difficult to access the values of private introspection and quiet character fostered in solitude, but the accompanying rise of consumer culture nurtured an anxiety associated with social isolation. It hardly needs to be argued that society today is only increasing in its speed and competitive intensity.

It is not only time that can reveal the conditioned nature of our degraded respect for solitude and the inner life. According to Cain, cultural differences—most often shaped by the contrast between so-called Western and Eastern philosophical approaches—reveal very different attitudes towards extroversion, introversion, and the value of solitude. Cain cites a study which compared "eight- to ten-year old children in Shanghai and southern Ontario, Canada." The study

> found that shy and sensitive children are shunned by their peers in Canada but make sought after playmates in China, where they are also more likely than other children to be considered for leadership roles. Chinese children who are sensitive and reticent are said to be *dongshi* (understanding), a common term of praise. (p. 187)

Explanations for this could include divergent attitudes towards education. In China, for example there is a long history of "reverence for education"

(p. 188) and success in education is made much easier if a good deal of time is dedicated to quiet, solitary study. Another reason offered in Cain's discussion is the emphasis in western culture in the individual in contrast to the eastern focus on the collective. The assertion of the ego results in the expression of the individual. As Cain states, as westerners "our destiny is to express ourselves, to follow our bliss, to be free of undue restraint, to achieve the one thing that we, and we alone, were brought into this world to do" (p. 189). This notion of the individual exists in a performative capacity and so requires outward expression and an ever-present audience as it competes for attention.

In her book, Cain presents an opportunity to consider our culture of extroversion in a different, more critical light. It is not necessary or even preferable to demonize extroversion; in its historical and cultural context, extroversion is understood for what it can contribute. But, as Cain makes clear, some rethinking of introversion must be undertaken for it becomes apparent that extroversion has not always been the preferred expression and it is not always the best approach especially when engaging with what I consider issues of central importance in our contemporary society. Issues such as peace, social justice, and responsibility for the natural world call for a return to collective and connective values that emerge in quiet reflection and restraint of the ego. Cain presents Gandhi as an eminent example of this:

> Experience has taught me that silence is part of the spiritual discipline of a votary of truth. We find so many people impatient to talk. All of this talking can hardly be said to be of any benefit to the world. It is so much a waste of time. My shyness has been in reality my shield and buckler. It has allowed me to grow. It has helped me in my discernment of truth. (Cited in Cain, 2013, p. 200)

BUDDHIST VIEWS ON SOLITUDE

In his study of the life of the Buddha, Buddhist scholar Trevor Ling illuminates a comparison of Susman's assessment of the impact of the western shift from a Culture of Character to a Culture of Personality to the social/political context of the teachings of the Buddha:

> The transition which many people were then experiencing from the familiar, small-scale society of old tribal republics to the strange, large-scale and consequently more impersonal, bleaker life of the new monarchical state, was accompanied by a psychological malaise, a heightened dissatisfaction with life as it had to be lived. It was this malaise which the Buddha was to take as his starting-point of his analysis of the human condition, calling it dukkha. (Cited in Sarvananda, 2012, p. 15)

Dukkha is commonly translated as "suffering" but Sarvananda makes clear in his book that the concept is more complex. It can be more accurately understood as "an uneasy sense of essential separateness," an "essential feeling of isolation and dissatisfaction" (p. 16) that can be understood as arising from an increased interaction with others in a more intensely individualized environment. Using the concept of dukkha, a concept fundamental to Buddhist practice, it is possible to mark the confusion that we seem to conjure up around our understanding of solitude. If the fundamental human fear is our experience of essential isolation, then it *seems* reasonable to repel all circumstances that require or encourage aloneness. We run in the opposite direction, toward the outward expression of connection with others, in the company of others. As we work to acquire substance in the outward world we add energy to the conditioned state that precipitated our sense of separateness in the first place.

Of course, we are creating our own dukkha by moving further and further away from an authentic connection with the unconditioned self which resides in emptiness of form and so an encompassing wholeness. As Sarvananda explains,

> ...samsara is that cyclic way of being in which our isolation is actually perpetuated by the mistaken belief that it can be removed by grasping at comfort, happiness, and security outside ourselves. The Buddha taught that we must cease to yearn for happiness outside ourselves and begin to trust the potential for nirvana that lies within us. The journey from samsara towards nirvana involves a passionate and deepening desire for a certain kind of self-sufficiency. (p. 23)

Buddhist understanding does more than simply allow us to embrace solitude in a new, more positive manner. It actually places solitude, aloneness, as fundamental to joyful, peaceful existence and realization of the full, authentic self. Self-sufficiency or "Self-Reliance," to draw on the words of Emerson, both allows and requires each person to know themselves and, in this knowing, express their full humanity. Solitude then creates the circumstance for a depth of connectivity to the self and through this, the whole. It is not a withdrawal; it is a return to a fundamental greatness if we conceive of "great" as an expression of our basic loving nature. As Emerson asserts, "It is easy in the world to live after the world's opinion; it is easy in solitude to live after your own; but the great man is he who in the midst of the crowd keeps with perfect sweetness the independence of solitude" ("Self-Reliance," 1841). From this we may come to understand that outward knowledge, positive civic contributions, and addressing important current social/political concerns—all things most educators would identify as primary goals in education—is not even possible without a recognition of the central importance of solitude and quiet in the lives of both students and teachers.

SOLITUDE IN TEACHING AND LEARNING

There are several concrete changes that this exploration has initiated in how I think about and plan to enact my position as teacher. I have affirmed the value I place in my own tendency towards introversion and in this have concluded that it is imperative that I make room for quiet and solitude in my regular work day. I will likely still struggle with the latent sense that attention to self is a mark of selfishness. This may be particularly difficult as a woman conditioned in a sexist society to accept a defining role of service to others. However, having had direct experience with collective benefits of my knowledge of self, arrived at through solitary contemplation, I can "reasonably" justify my choice.

I will pay attention to how much I talk, and I will discipline myself to maintain silence as often as I can. This will be far more difficult for me because I have been widely affirmed in my role as "speaker." I am still trying to come to terms with myself as an educator and as a teacher leader who does not lead through the sheer "force of personality." Meditation and the solitude it requires will slowly unfold, more and more, the soft power of silence. Staff meetings and classroom discussions will now become an opportunity to practice mindful silence.

Most importantly, I have come to a new understanding of students in my classroom and the negative impact blind adherence to ministry expectations in English may be having on them. It may seem small but I have experienced a radical shift in how I identify and value class participation and presentation skills. In this it may be worth a bit of passive resistance against department policy. I want to directly explore with my students the values we place on extroversion and introversion, actively question our assumptions, and permit more independent, introspective demonstration of this critique in place of demonstrating assumed necessary skills in public speaking.

I will use group work differently and I will ensure space for independent thinking and working. This is not a strategy that is only intended to increase the comfort and safety of more introverted students; it is also a recognition that solitary work and thought is fundamental to my goals as a teacher, to the rights of the student to have their knowledge of self prioritized and protected in the educational system.

Holistic education presents a challenge to the current structures of education employed in most mainstream systems in North America; it poses important questions about the how and why of what we do in our classrooms and presents an opportunity to teach and learn differently, with more authentic, human oriented goals in mind. The nature of this challenge, as fitting for the fundamentals of holistic education, is quiet and organic. In my opinion, there will be no Holistic Revolution, but I would also assert that this is no reason to feel disheartened. Much of my career has been spent struggling to improve conditions for my students through a rethinking and redesign of the system we work within. I have been searching for ways to explain, for research to support, for reports to justify. Most of my efforts that I would have identified as effective have been about the outward energy I can expend and have not taken care or advantage of my strengths as an introvert, have not honored the potential in "cease[ing] to yearn for happiness outside ourselves and begin[ning] to trust the potential for nirvana that lies within us" (Sarvananda, 2012, p. 23). Meditation or creating space for quiet reflection will not resolve the very real limitations and often harmful consequences of our current educational structures but what it can do is allow educators an opportunity to access a fullness of self that makes radical, rooted change conceivable. In those moments of solitude when "unfolds, emerges, what I am" (Larkin), possible new ways of being also emerge, and from the inside out meaningful educational change may be realized.

REFERENCES

Cain, S. (2013). *Quiet: The power of introverts in a world that can't stop talking.* New York, NY: Random House Publishing.

Sarvananda. (2012). *Solitude and loneliness: A Buddhist view.* Cambridge: Windhorse Publications.

CHAPTER 19

MY LIFE AS EDUCATOR AS SHAPED BY LIFE EXPERIENCE

Nyambura Kariuki
University of Toronto

THE BEGINNINGS OF A SOUND EDUCATIONAL BASE

I was born in Kenya and began my formal education there when I was five years old. Later that year, my family moved to Missouri, where we lived for seven years. We are exposed to teachers, be they parents, schoolteachers, friends, or siblings. The encouragement I received from my parents enabled me to deal with the challenges I experienced in both the Kenyan and American school systems. I had access to books, tutors, and other amenities I needed for school. My parents' involvement laid a foundation for success and the beginning of a solid education.

Exemplary teachers have also played a major part in my life. Mrs. Buster, my grade four teacher was exceptional. She was caring, generous, smart, and approachable. She developed a strong sense of community-mindedness in each student and this contributed to the well-being of the whole classroom. I was a new student from a foreign country with very little English, but her warmth and personality alleviated my fears and enabled me to

Teaching From the Thinking Heart, pages 171–178
Copyright © 2014 by Information Age Publishing
171

learn more effectively. Mrs. Buster's holistic approach allowed me to feel safe and comfortable in this learning environment and gave me a sense of belonging.

My experience with my Kenyan primary school teacher was very different. My classroom teacher was intimidating and often made sarcastic remarks to many of her students. I was fearful of approaching her or doing anything wrong. I would regularly come home in low spirits, begging my parents to move me to another class. I survived the year with my parents' support and extra tutoring lessons, as I was not learning in the class. As a result, I developed a passionate belief about the importance of creating a caring and loving atmosphere for children to be able to learn.

These two school experiences led me to understand that a student's success is based largely on the relationship between the teacher and learner. This relationship must not only be reciprocal and empathetic for the learner's needs; it needs to go hand in hand with a genuine interest on the part of the teacher to help develop the student's identity and knowledge base (Patel, 2003).

After studying anthropology in university, I became involved in various types of informal teaching. I taught Sunday school from primary to high school in both Kenya and the United States. I have been exposed to a diverse group of people, young and old and a wide variety of nationalities. I had the privilege of working as an ESL teacher with a Korean ESL community in Toronto. Many times, I worried that I was not doing a good job, but my students' attention and willingness to learn encouraged me. They shared common values of being caring, approachable, and open to learning. Educators need to establish in their classroom and atmosphere where the students and teachers can be co-learners together. Gone are the days where we exist solely to teach students. We must not be afraid when learning goes beyond our own knowledge base. For the true teacher, pedagogy must be something living and new, not memorized or already worked out (Holistic Education Tasmania, 1997).

After these experiences, I made the decision to become a counselor. I felt I could make a difference in people's lives by being a better listener and offering hope where I could. These skills would be a great benefit in my more formal teaching years, particularly in the ability to spot signs of stress or distress where communication was limited.

Halfway through my counseling career (I was a counselor for two years in a program conducted by the Toronto School of Theology), my professor said to me, "I think you would make a great teacher seeing how you speak of working with children so often." His encouragement sparked me to apply to teacher's college. I was both nervous and excited at the same time as I began my teaching career. I realized then that all my life experiences had led to this point, shaping my personality and philosophy of teaching.

Fred Korthagen (2004) points out the way the teachers see their role is to a large extent colored by the events and individuals in their lives. Hamachek (1999) advises that the more that teachers know about themselves the more their personal decisions are apt to be about how to pave the way for better teaching. This inner knowledge is otherwise known as the private curriculum. As I reflect about what to teach the children and how to do it, I have often steered away from following a rigid curriculum and engaged in teaching that is directed by the inquiry and further exploration of the students themselves. This leads to a more fulfilling experience for the students in school.

INCORPORATION—A HOLISTIC WORLDVIEW IN MY PROFESSION

According to Dewey, "education is not a preparation for life, it is life itself" (Dewey, 1916). Dewey suggests that learning goes beyond the four walls of the classroom. In other words, one is always learning throughout life. All our experiences formal or informal should serve to help students to integrate into the community. Hence Dewey's perspective: learning is life, and life is learning. With this in mind, I came to understand how my past, present, and future experiences shape me as an educator.

As I began my new career as an elementary teacher, I was filled with many questions. Would I be an effective teacher? How would I ensure all my students are learning? How could I build a strong sense of community in my class? Would I be able to teach the whole curriculum? How could I make learning fun? Although teacher's college had given me the theoretical tools I needed, it was in the classroom where I learned to be a teacher. I discovered how relevant it was for classroom learning to be integrated with experiential learning in order to provide relevant and meaningful resources to help students succeed. When the students are engaged in taking initiative, making decisions, and being accountable, their learning becomes more authentic. Experiential learning involves hands-on, collaborative, and reflective learning experience which helps the students to incorporate new knowledge and skills. At each stage the students are engaging with their classmates and instructor simultaneously. The ultimate test lies in their ability to be able to apply what they have learned to another situation.

Korthagen (2004) suggests teachers who have spent years as students in school develop their own beliefs about teaching. He discovered that many of these beliefs are diametrically opposed to those presented during their teacher education, especially in relation to classroom structure, where ensuring students' own contribution to the learning process becomes crucial. Teachers hold beliefs about what they believe in relation to curriculum, colleagues, and students. This also includes perceived strengths and weaknesses, values, self-efficacy, and matters about which they feel responsible for. A major point of departure today from traditional learning is the emphasis on constructivist teaching methods, which focuses on teachers' and children's sense making. Teachers are called upon to relinquish singular claims to authority or power in the classroom.

BROOKMEDE PUBLIC SCHOOL

My first principal at Brookmede exemplified what it meant to be both a leader and educator. Aware of my inhibitions as a new teacher, she put me at ease by placing me with a grade three teacher mentor who ensured that I had access to supplies and teaching resources. The principal would often check in with me to see how she could support me. She reminded me of the core concept of caring for the whole child in the classroom by endeavoring to know each child personally, creating a safe environment and ensuring justice for everyone. She offered an example of holistic education where the development of the whole person—body, mind, and spirit is the focus (J. Miller, 2007).

The school year was not without its challenges. Trying to make sense of the curriculum documents was difficult. How was I to get through all of it? I had to quickly learn about the art of integrating subjects and how to choose topics relevant to the students. So much attention in our educational system is focused on the intellect, and the body, emotions, and spirit can sometimes be neglected (J. Miller, 2007).

This is revealed by standardized testing like EQAO (Education Quality and Accountability Office) tests which are based on a very narrow definition of accountability. Over four years of teaching grade three, I often put aside fun learning activities in order to accommodate EQAO testing preparation. Recently, however, surveys done by ETFO (The Elementary Teachers' Federation of Ontario) show most teachers do not find standardized tests scores very useful (Dasko, 2010). Good teacher observation, documentation of student work, and performance-based assessment, which involve direct evaluation of real learning tasks, provide a more authentic assessment and provide useful feedback to the students.

Ron Miller (2005) identifies our modern culture as technocratic. He argues our current culture does not trust organic functioning but prefers to implement proven, standardized techniques and methods. Our first task then is to escape the limitations of a technocratic way of thinking (R. Miller, 2005) and promote a more authentic pedagogy—which involves ways of teaching and learning that are harmonious with the natural rhythms of human development. Such pedagogy corresponds to the developmental phases of childhood and nurtures the child's creativity and free thinking in a school environment. It recognizes the individuality of the whole child. The benefits of a more holistic perspective extend beyond the academic curriculum and with the understanding that every person's intelligence and abilities are far more complex than his or her scores on standardized tests. It goes further to enable each person to find identity, meaning, and purpose in life through connections to the community, to the natural world, and to spiritual values such as compassion and peace.

Assessment can be valuable when it does not separate students into performance categories, but rather helps students better understand their own growth (O'Grady & Alwis, 2012). Students can learn to be accountable and learn to cultivate creative thinking, flexible problem solving, and collaboration, the skills they need to be successful in work and life. Indeed, individuals learn better when what is being learned is important to them.

What is the best way to teach outside the test then? In my classroom, I made it a priority during September to focus on building a strong classroom community. Such a classroom enables the children to feel connected to others, enabling the teachers to address children's basic needs, promote their resilience to hardship, and teach the values of respect and responsibility while fostering their social and academic competence. Scott Forbes (1996) in *Values in Holistic Education* reinforces that all relationships are important: relationships between students, between teachers, and between students and teachers are seen as both a primary source and topic of education.

THORNWOOD PUBLIC SCHOOL

Nurturing the soul is educating the heart (J. Miller, 2010). As teachers we need to recognize that students' attitudes and emotions need nurturing during the learning process. During my third year of teaching grade three, Robert walked into my life and taught me what it meant for a teacher to nurture a student's soul. He had a beautiful smile which often masked what was going on inside. He was from a single parent home and showed signs of insecurity. He rarely let his guard down, acting tough no matter what was happening.

The first few months were full of violent episodes. Robert would often act out using crude language, throwing chairs, and intimidating the other students and me. I needed support from the administration, which was readily available. I learned how to become more patient, although there were times when I felt I wouldn't be able to get through a lesson or the day. Despite all these challenges, I had to learn to reach out to Robert. He needed to know that I cared for him beyond the classroom walls, and that I could be trusted. I worked hard to ensure Robert, and the rest of the students received the support they needed to be successful. The hard work paid off, and towards the end of the school year, Robert and I had a meaningful relationship.

We must provide the right conditions and allow the students to grow up to be who they really are—spiritual beings with the natural right to become integrated, intelligent, ethical, and therefore mature, responsible, and civilized adults able to cooperate peacefully and effectively in their efforts to resolve their human problems. In effect, we must provide universal education for complete human development or 'holistic' education. (Holistic Education Tasmania, 2012).

It was important for Robert that I base his education and learning experience on his individual need for wholeness. He could then continue to gain a sense of identity, meaning, and purpose in life through connections with the community and the natural world (J. Miller, 2007). This situation enabled me to have a better understanding of the individual person and how all of us are intrinsically connected to social, cultural, biological, and spiritual environments to become more whole within ourselves (Holistic Education Tasmania, 2012).

HOLISTIC EDUCATION FOR LIFE

Teachers should be lifelong learners, updating content knowledge as well as refining and revising their understanding of teaching. The primary job of education is to teach one to ask questions, and the secondary job involves praising that action. This issue of how we should teach is still prevalent in today's society. Martin Luther King, Jr. (1947) writes, "The function of education, therefore, is to teach one to think intensively and to think critically. But education which stops with efficiency may prove the greatest menace to society." By engaging students through discovery, analysis, and interactive learning, they learn the necessary skills or tools to become valuable members of society. When education allows students to interact with others from different backgrounds and study events from different perspectives, they are able to learn to work with people who differ from them. Without cooperation, understanding, critical thinking, and learning our nation and world would not be able to function (Patel, 2003, p. 15).

Primarily, teachers must strive to make learning interactive and stimulating to the students. The students must become owners of their knowledge and this ownership of knowledge underpins the holistic approach (Patel, 2003). One strategy that builds on meaningful teaching and acquisition of knowledge is to co-construct criteria for assessment with the students. This has brought about a deeper understanding and more student engagement in my classroom.

The interaction between the teacher and the student needs to encompass the personal, professional, and social requirements of the learner. More than to gain knowledge, these requirements oblige a student to be heard, praised, and accepted into the community of learners. A holistic teacher develops a student into an inspired person by using teaching devices to raise their confidence, urging them to consider the relevance of knowledge to the self (Patel, 2003, p. 10). At the core of the "whole child" concept is the understanding that children grow physically, emotionally, and intellectually; therefore, school should attend to all of these areas of growth.

All teachers hold beliefs about the purpose of schooling. For some teachers, these beliefs are rooted in a holistic perspective wherein the purpose of education is to help all children reach their full potential in every facet of their lives. More than anything else, empowerment of our students, our concern for their humanity, helps them to integrate into the world around them.

REFERENCES

Dasko, D. (2010, August). Teachers' views of standardized testing and eqao. Paper presented to elementary Teachers Federation of Ontario, from: http://www.etfo.ca/IssuesinEducation/EQAOTesting/TeachersViews/Documents/Teachers_Views_EQAO.pdf

Dewey, J. (1916). *Democracy and education.* Retrieved from: http://www.schoolofeducators.com/wp-content/uploads/2011/12/EXPERIENCE-EDUCATION-JOHN-DEWEY.pdf

Hamachek, D. (1999). Effective teachers: What they do, how they do it, and the importance of self-knowledge. *The role of self in teacher development,* 189.

Holistic Education Tasmania: (1997, July). *Spirituality in education conference quotes* Retrieved from: Newshttp://www.hent.org/july97/quotes.htm

Forbes, S. H. (1996, June). Values in holistic education. In *Third Annual Conference on 'Education, Spirituality and the Whole Child', Roehampton Institute London.*

Future schools and education as the practice of freedom for growth through learning. (n.d.). Retrieved from http://www.holisticeducator.com/holisticeducation.htm

King, Jr. M. L. (1947). The purpose of education. *Martin Luther King, Research & Education Institute.* Retrieved from: http://mlk-kpp01.stanford.edu/index.php/encyclopedia/documentsentry/doc_470200_000/

Korthagen, F. (2004). In search of the essence of a good teacher: Towards a more holistic approach in teacher education. *Teaching and Teacher Education 20*(1), 77–97.

Miller, J. (2010). *Whole child education.* Toronto: U. of Toronto Press.

Miller, J. (2007). *The holistic curriculum.* Toronto: U. of Toronto Press.

Miller, R. (2005, November). *Holistic education: A response to the crisis of our time.* Presented at the Institute for Values Education in Istanbul, Turkey. Retrieved from: http://www.pathsoflearning.net/articles_Holistic_Ed_Response.php

O'Grady, G., & Alwis, W. A. M. (2012). Holistic assessment and problem-based learning. In *One-day, one-problem* (pp. 187–212). Springer Singapore.

Patel, N. V. (2003). A holistic approach to learning and teaching interaction: factors in the development of critical learners. *International Journal of Educational Management, 17*(6), 272–284.

CHAPTER 20

JUST LOVE

Learning about Listening, Giving, and Forgiving

Maria Karmiris
University of Toronto

"Fads in education will come and go. The only thing you need to remember is to just love the children. Just love them. That is all that matters." These were the words spoken to me by a retired teacher who was a customer at a fruit market where I worked during my undergraduate years at university. I was seriously considering pursuing teaching as a career. My family and friends perceived it as a good choice since teaching is considered a stable and secure profession. Even though my family and friends knew me best, it was indeed the words of this kind stranger that resonated with me, and that I have repeatedly recalled during my teaching career.

While it is true there is a perception of teaching as being stable, safe, and secure, these are not the attributes that were most appealing to me 11 years ago when I began my teaching career. What appealed to me most was the potential for transformation. According to Miller, "deep change comes from the heart" (2007, p. 91).

Teaching From the Thinking Heart, pages 179–185
Copyright © 2014 by Information Age Publishing

In her work, *All about Love: New Visions*, bell hooks uses M. Scott Peck's definition of love as a guidepost for the inherent power of love to transform:

> Love [is] the will to extend one's self for the purpose of nurturing one's own or another's spiritual growth...Love is as love does. Love is an act of will— namely, both an intention and an action. Will also implies choice. We do not have to love. We choose to love. (hooks, 2000, p. 4)

Love is an active choice that may manifest itself in different places, ways, and forms but has the ultimate intention of nurturing the best that is in us and in others. As Miller (2010) describes in his work, transformational education is not static or rigid in its structure, but rather it is fluid: "Instead of seeing the school as a factory where people behave as if working on an assembly line, the school can be seen as a complex living organism—changing through a sense of purpose, collaboration and deep sense of inner direction" (Miller, 2010, p. 91). Teaching with heart encompasses an element of reverence for life in all its wondrous forms. To paraphrase both hooks (2000) and Miller (2010), infusing teaching with love is an active process that is responsive to the needs of our students for the purpose of effecting positive change and outcomes.

I have always aspired to teach with heart in the hopes of affecting change in the lives of others, yet, eleven years ago, I did not realize the depths of love I would encounter in moments of loving kindness. According to Miller, "If we see ourselves as connected to others, then compassion arises naturally, since we do not see ourselves separate from other beings" (2010 p. 30). A similar sentiment is echoed in the work of Paul Tillich (1954) who expresses his belief that it is through creating the bonds of community with each other that we need to maintain a balance between love, power, and justice.

> The relation of justice to love...can adequately be described through three functions of creative justice, namely, listening, giving, and forgiving. In none of them does love do more than justice demands, but in each of them love recognizes what justice demands. (Tillich, 1954, p. 84)

If we seek to sustain, nurture, and transform our relationships with each other and our communities through love then we simultaneously need to be committed to justice; a justice that seeks to uphold love through "...listening, giving, and forgiving."

I have come to realize how full these 11 years have been with countless moments of compassion and loving kindness that embody the functions of justice as moments of listening, moments of giving, and moments of forgiving as outlined by Tillich. I believe it is through building connections and nurturing each other that we uncover opportunities for transformative moments in teaching and learning that truly embody the importance of listening, giving, and forgiving.

LISTENING

In order to know what is just in a person-to-person encounter,
love listens. It is its first task to listen.
—Tillich, 1954, p. 84

During my first year of teaching, I met "Mary-Anne," a fifth grade student in my class who seemed to greet each day and opportunity for learning with great joy and enthusiasm. I never would have known or guessed that Mary-Anne was living in a home where she may have experienced physical abuse, as reported by her younger sister. Mary-Anne displayed all the attributes of being a happy, well-adjusted sociable child. It shocked me when Mary-Anne and her sister were removed from the school by CAS (Children's Aid Society) and temporarily placed in foster care. Several weeks later, Mary-Anne returned to school under the temporary custody of her aunt. She came back to class with the same big smile she always had but with a sadness in her eyes she could not hide. The first morning, she asked if she could stay in for recess instead of going out to play. As the last students left the class, I asked her if she was okay. As the tears streamed down her face, she said, "It is hard being back. I feel embarrassed. I miss my mom. I just want to go home." I felt helpless in the realization that I could not fix the problems in this child's life. I did not have any answers for her. I had no words that could help ease her pain, her sorrow, and her unneeded sense of shame. All I was able to do was be present in her sadness. I looked her in the eyes and patted her back. I still wish that I could have done more. I still wonder if what I did was enough. I stood beside my student and was present in her sadness, and I connected with her by listening.

That moment of helplessness and sorrow transformed me as an educator in two significant ways. First, the memory serves as a constant reminder that as teachers we barely scratch the surface of understanding the inner or outer life of our students. The glimpse of Mary-Anne's inner world during that morning recess left me both speechless and in awe of how little I understood the hearts and minds of the children I was teaching. This feeling of awe and humility is something that I have experienced repeatedly as a teacher.

Miller (2010) contends that an important component in developing dialogue in our school communities is the embodiment of humility. In quoting the work of Paulo Freire he writes:

> Dialogue cannot exist without humility ... Dialogue as the encounter of human beings addressed to the common task of learning and acting, is broken if the parties (or one of them) lack humility. How can I dialogue if I always project ignorance onto others and never perceive my own? At the point of encounter ... there are only people who are attempting together, to learn more than they now know. (p. 157)

Each time I am reminded of how little I know and how much I need to learn, I feel deeply humbled and I hope more open to savoring the present moment and every opportunity it provides to learn from a student, a colleague, or a parent. Miller (2007) reminds us that being present in every interaction with a student is the most "critical" component in fully attending, listening, and responding to the needs of our students (pp. 190–195). Listening with the intention of learning from another is fundamental in our efforts to build community through dialogue in our schools.

Mary-Anne's story also transformed me as an educator in developing the heartbreaking understanding that the children we teach often feel a needless sense of shame for a myriad of injustices that are not their fault. bell hooks (2000) reminds us of the right of every child irrespective of class, race, or gender to justice.

> Love is as love does, and it is our responsibility to give children love. When we love children we acknowledge by our every action that they are not property, that they have rights—that we respect and uphold their rights. Without justice there can be no love. (p. 30)

hooks suggests that as adults our actions, words, and deeds hold enormous power to wound, or nurture and heal the hearts and minds of the children we are entrusted to guide and inspire. Her passionate plea for the right to justice of all human beings including children is also echoed in the words of Tillich over fifty years ago.

> All things and all men, so to speak, call on us with small or loud voices. They want us to listen, they want us to understand their intrinsic claims, their justice of being. They want justice from us. But we can give it to them only through the love which listens. (p. 84)

Countless students, like Mary-Anne, have called on me to listen to their voices. I hope in my own small way that I have been able to give them exactly what they have asked for, a listening and compassionate heart.

GIVING

Thousands of candles can be lighted from a single candle, and the life of the candle will not be shortened. Happiness never decreases by being shared."
—Buddha

It was in my seventh year of teaching when my encounter with "Sofia" would serve to transform my sense of building and nurturing community in the classroom due to her unending ability to give from her heart. At the time, I was teaching grade three and Sofia was assigned to be the Special Needs Assistant (SNA) for two students with physical disabilities that were a part of my classroom that year. Sofia had been the SNA for these two students since they were in grade one and as a result she had built an incredible rapport with "Ahmed" and "Rohan" and their families. Sofia was not only an incredible source of support for both of these boys, she selflessly helped me gain a better understanding of the particular strengths and needs of these two children as we worked together to ensure their inclusion into our classroom community.

We were all deeply heartbroken in January of that school year when the doctors discovered that "Ahmed" had a brain tumor and would need to have surgery. Our class created cards of good wishes and hope for a speedy recovery. The staff at our school knit a quilt for him and collected money for the family to help with additional expenses. Though different members of our school community gave whatever they could, Sofia gave from the depths of her heart.

Periodically, I went to visit Ahmed and his family at Sick Kids and subsequently at Holland-Bloorview, but Sofia remained committed to the well-being of Ahmed and his family by visiting Ahmed in the hospital almost weekly and visiting the family at home, too. When anyone at school needed an update on Ahmed's condition we knew we could rely on Sofia for the most recent information. After Ahmed's long recovery, he was no longer able to walk and as a result was placed at a different school that could manage his needs. Sofia organized a visit to Ahmed's new school where the two of us went with two of Ahmed's closest friends. When it was time to leave, Rohan kneeled in front of Ahmed's wheelchair and spoke to Ahmed's legs. He said, "I hope you feel better soon so that you can walk again." Ahmed looked at his friend and said quietly and gently, "My legs aren't going to get better. This is how I am now." Sometimes, teachers bear witness to such profound moments of compassionate love between others that they cannot help to feel anything but blessed. I was able to experience that moment of tenderness because of Sofia and her deep connection to the students she was assigned to support.

bell hooks reminds us that "the heart of justice is truth telling, seeing ourselves and the world the way it is rather than the way we want it to be" (2000, p. 33). Our society tends to marginalize people based on a variety of factors such as race, gender, and socio-economic status. Sofia's intention, in her quiet commitment to developing and nurturing connections with students and their families, drew my attention to how our communities also marginalize people with special needs. When we are building community within our schools and our classrooms, every voice matters. In writing about the importance of social justice bell hooks states, "...loving practice is not aimed at simply giving an individual greater life satisfaction; it is extolled as the primary way we end domination and oppression" (p. 76). Miller (2010) expresses a similar understanding of the need for justice in our communities when referring to Dr. Martin Luther King's concept of a "beloved" community: "Each person owes a debt to others for survival and for the existence of society and should be aware that an injustice done to one person or group of people is an injustice to all human beings" (p. 81). Sofia knew this intuitively and lived this philosophy every day in the way she listened with her heart and gave with her spirit.

FORGIVING

Forgiveness is an act of generosity.
—hooks, 2000, p. 139

Recalling these moments of compassionate love in my teaching career is particularly healing at this moment and time. The last few years have been the most challenging of my career. It has been such a challenging time because I have felt disconnected from my work. I have taken on more responsibilities than I could have conceived at the start of my career. Despite working for endless hours on various projects, committees, clubs, and events I have felt less rewarded, less joyful, and less connected to my career and to my students. Recently, I have been plagued by self-doubt, self-criticism, and the perpetual feeling that I will never be able to give enough to make a difference. Sometimes, the biggest injustice or disservice a person can do is by being overly critical, demanding, and unforgiving of their own self. In the midst of trying to listen and give whatever I could to the students and school community, I forgot to take the time to listen to myself.

This feeling of hopelessness, disconnection, and loss was exactly the space I was in at the end of June in my tenth year of teaching, when a student I taught in my second year of teaching walked towards me in the school hallway with his arms open and gave me hug. "Shrey" now a young man was visiting Toronto from Phoenix, Arizona where he was a student at Arizona State University studying civil engineering. He was glad to see me because he wanted to say thank you.

I was stunned. When this young man was a ten year old boy in my class, there were many moments when he would sit at his desk and cry. I never did get to the bottom of his crying. While he was in my class and from time to time after he moved on, I worried about him. I was always under the impression that he disliked my class, but he assured me that his tears had nothing to do with my class. He said: "I wanted to tell you that you are one of the best teachers I ever had because I knew you cared about me and wanted the best for me." I am grateful to him for helping me to see the glimmer of hope in my own work at a time when I most needed to be reminded of the power of connections lovingly made and nurtured with kindness.

I am also grateful to him for helping me to see the importance of forgiving myself and forgiving others. As educators we bear witness to and attempt to rectify the systemic injustices which affect the lives of our students and our communities. From the seemingly minor playground heartbreaks that are a source of momentary tears and hurt to the much larger wounds and scars caused by the perpetuation of oppressive hierarchies, it is easy to become overwhelmed with a sense of frustration with the problems we encounter.

> Realistically, being part of a loving community does not mean we will not face conflicts, betrayals, negative outcomes from positive actions, or bad things happening to good people. Love allows us to confront these negative realities in a manner that is life-affirming and life enhancing...Forgiveness is an act of generosity...By forgiving we clear a path on the way to love. It is a gesture or respect. (hooks, 2000, p. 139)

To recommit myself to the goal of nurturing my students, I needed to forgive myself for feeling that I could never do or give enough to truly make a difference. Shrey's message of gratitude helped me to understand that it is enough to greet each moment as an opportunity to connect with the heart of another human being. Through forgiveness, Shrey helped me to reconnect with hope. He helped me to believe again that our efforts as educators to seek the best in ourselves and in others is a fruitful process. Practicing forgiveness helped me to find hope again and to understand its necessity to building loving and nurturing communities.

Miller writes, "Clearly there is a mystery to teaching and being aware of this mystery is truly humbling" (2010, p. 99). I felt humbled by Shrey's visit because often when experiencing moments of connection with students, colleagues, or parents, I have felt more like the student than the teacher. I remain unsure if anything I have done has had a transformative effect on my students. I do know that my time connecting with my students has transformed me. I am aware that the moments of greatest significance to me do not revolve around any of the content, facts, or strategies that I have taught. What I remember most are those moments of connection with others. Being open to changing my mind, feeling an overwhelming sense of loving kindness, and sustaining a sense of hope that comes with developing a sense of community is what teaching with heart means to me.

REFERENCES

hooks, b. (2000). *all about love: New Visions.* New York: Harper Collins Publishers.

Miller, J. (2007). *The holistic curriculum.* Toronto: University of Toronto Press.

Miller, J. (2010). *Whole child education.* Toronto: University of Toronto Press.

Tillich, P. (1954). *Love, power and justice.* London: Oxford University Press.

CHAPTER 21

MY HOLISTIC JOURNEY

Significant Moments of a Lifelong Learner and Educator

Christopher Russell
University of Toronto

PROLOGUE

I am a son. I am a husband. I am a father. I am a friend. I am blessed. I am a teacher. I am a student. I am both fair and unfair. I am White. I am a pain in the arse. I am a joker. I am privileged. I am insensitive. I am blind. I am kind. I am polite. I am respectful.

Like anyone with a heartbeat, or someone whose time on Earth has come to pass, I am a myriad of things to both others and myself. Family and friends are important to me.

For the purpose of this paper I want you to know that I also consider myself a geographer, a poet, a photographer, and a music lover. It is through these artistic mediums that I find comfort in trying to make sense of the complex worlds within and around me. These mediums also help me relate to the world in a holistic fashion, thus enabling me to feel more deeply in tune.

Teaching From the Thinking Heart, pages 187–193

I formally began my career in teaching back in 1996, with the East York Board of Education. Since then, I have been fortunate to gain experience in public and private schools, teaching both coed and single-sex students from grades 1–6. I currently teach grade 6 at a small and dynamic private school in Toronto, Ontario called The Mabin School.

The following is part of the story of my holistic journey as a person and learner, as well as an educator—past, present, and future . . . mind, body, and spirit.

THE PAST: IT'S THERE, BENEATH THE SURFACE

Senility

It had been a lovely afternoon
bounding over the ice-floes of Indian harbour with my father,
picnicking with my love on the primeval shores of my birthplace, Bay Roberts
Newfoundland.
The healing sound of Atlantic Water,
the fresh bouquet of cod
intensified the landscape's beauty.
Now, to my frustration
the sun's position heightens the shadows of my youth
forcing me to drift more swiftly,
back to where the terrain and azure are drastic.
An alarming divide
where the land is depressed
the welkin dreary.
Unlike the Past,
the Present is neither decorative nor, at times, familiar.
It's landscape is cruel and each landmark often senseless.
As incongruous as the mottled oxbow-shapes
that interrupt the floodplain,
therein the valley spread before me.
Like the geography of land
my memory
is inconstant.
Its landscape altered by the passing of ages

—Christopher Russell, 1994

The poem above is a tribute to my late grandfather, on my father's side. His name was Harvey Winston Russell and he was a proud and resourceful Newfoundlander. Eventually, he immigrated from "the rock" to Toronto. Regrettably, I wasn't very close to my grandfather even though he resided in Leaside, while I lived and grew up in nearby Don Mills. The Euclidean space between us was the distance of a mere twelve-minute drive. But, sadly the emotional distance between him and our family was much greater. He was a hard man with invisible demons. Later in his life he suffered from dementia, which added another layer to an already complex being.

However, if you looked or listened carefully, in quieter less guarded moments, a glint of something intangible emanated from him. I believe it was his soul. This glint sometimes surfaced when he and I shared a rare pot of tea, saltine crackers, and white, extra old cheddar cheese at his dining room table. To this day, I think of him when these simple but comforting morsels visit my palette. This glint surfaced behind a faraway gaze back into the distance, where his mind desperately swam the currents of time to search for and cling to patches of memory from his youth.

The poem *Senility* is significant in terms of holism in that it too is concerned with connections in human experience: connections between mind and body, between linear and intuitive ways of knowing, between individual and community, and between the personal self and the transpersonal self (Miller, 2007). It also addresses the effect that life's experiences can have upon us along with the imprint that is left behind, particularly during our formative years.

From my parents I have learned many things, such as manners, the importance of family and friends, the value of hard work and perseverance. My mother and father also helped me to try and see the beauty, strength, courage, and the potential in both people and places even when they are not immediately apparent. They taught me to listen and question with care and courage; to watch and act with an open mind and heart; and they taught me that there is much one can learn and do in a lifetime.

I am humbled and grateful for all the things they have shared with me throughout my life.

When I look back over my life, I realize that the most powerful and memorable learning experiences I've encountered were ones that transformed me in some way. Generally, these transformative moments were life lessons learned beyond the walls of my traditional and predominantly transmission-oriented public school education in the 1970s and 1980s. Such memorable moments exposed me to a deeper sense of connectedness to people, myself, and the world around me. To me, in essence, these moments were holistic in nature. As Miller (2007) puts it, when discussing relationships to the soul, these memorable moments fostered a "sense of inclusion and connection" (p. 14) within me.

Such holistic moments from my past include summers spent at camp as a camper, counselor and canoe instructor; cooking with my mother, volunteering at various community events, or welcoming someone to our neighborhood with her; walking, talking, watching, and listening in the woods with my father, or interacting with homeless people up Yonge Street in Toronto on a Saturday night with him. Upon reflection, these experiences helped, in significant part, to shape who I am and how I interact with others.

Ultimately, love was a guiding principle in each of the aforementioned holistic and memorable moments from my past. In many ways I relate to, and concur with, the thoughts of bell hooks in Carl Leggo's (2011) article titled "Living Love: Confessions of a Fearful Teacher" when "what matters" in a classroom is considered:

> Love in the classroom prepares teachers and students to open our minds and hearts. It is the foundation on which every learning community can be created. Teachers need not fear that practicing love in the classroom will lead to favoritism. Love will always move us away from domination in all its forms. Love will always challenge and change us. This is the heart of the matter. (p. 137)

THE PRESENT: FEEL MORE

A Gift From the Orcas

Beneath a majestic infinity
atop a salty abyss,
I beheld the natural beauty of the orcas

Heard their songs immaculate
felt their magical aura

Like aquatic gypsies
these tireless travelers
moved gently to the sea

leaving me with
something I had lost—

my childlike sense of wonder

—Christopher Russell, 1993

Wonder. The older I get, the more I realize the importance of having wonder in one's life. The courage to wonder; the wisdom to share and inspire wonder; and the tenacity to seek and unearth wonder are truly priceless gifts.

As a father, I am constantly in awe of my children's abilities to wonder. I often can't keep up to their innocent and heartfelt queries as they try to navigate their ever-changing world. Similarly, with my students, I am often amazed by their seemingly limitless ability to wonder about their social, emotional, and intellectual worlds. Hence, holistic learning is inspirational to me in that it supports wonder and joy through tending to all aspects of the person—body, mind, and spirit.

Wonder, joy, and compassion are supported in my classroom through emergent learning and inquiry, the use of documentation, and service-learning. These teaching methods are all examples of ways I try to more deeply connect with my students, as well as create curricular experiences that can lead them closer to some form of personal transformation. For the purpose of this paper, I will solely focus on the merits of service-learning and its ability to holistically foster relationship between self and community. Also, for the purpose of this paper, service-learning is defined as the "integration of academic learning with meeting the community's needs to the benefits of both students and community" (Donahue, 1999, p. 685).

In my experience, I believe that service-learning is a powerful vehicle to engage students, teach them empathy, and make powerful connections that can ultimately transform them. As Miller (2006) writes, "Engaged service, then, is a process of attempting to heal this suffering in others and ourselves" (p. 70). Recently, over the last few years, I have worked with colleagues, families, and people beyond our school community to engage grade 6 private school students in community experiences that are deeply linked to curricular expectations and, in their essence, are holistic. Stemming from emergent investigations of Canadian trade, child poverty, and immigration, I have had my class connect with a school in one of the most challenged socioeconomic communities in Toronto, while a different group of students decided to donate their time and energy to supporting the work of the Daily Bread Food Bank.

From these community service experiences, many of the students expressed a deeper sense of empathy. They also displayed greater levels of wonder and joy from becoming involved in their communities and developing relationships with people connected to issues that affect others and themselves.

Donahue (1999) acknowledges Kahne and Westheimer (1996), stating that it is important to understand different forms of service-learning: 'charity' versus 'change'. Donahue (1999) writes: "According to these authors, teachers using service-learning oriented towards charity emphasize giving–helping others and countering self-centeredness" (p. 687). Alternatively, "...teachers using service-learning oriented towards change emphasize caring over giving–developing reciprocal relationships with the persons they are serving, apprehending the reality of the persons being served, and building a greater sense of community" (p. 687). To me, there is value in both forms of service-learning, however, it is important to not mistake or interchange them. In either case though, one must proceed with care and actively listen to the persons they are serving so that the service experience is helpful and not detrimental.

Early into a classroom assignment that supported grade 6 service work, students were challenged to hypothetically meet their basic needs. Specifically, they were to find food and shelter on either current welfare rates or via a minimum wage job at McDonald's. Deeper into this project, one student perceptively wrote:

I cannot believe how some refugees, immigrants, and poor people in Toronto live. They really can only afford to have the essentials. They're constantly budgeting whenever they want to buy something because they have to have enough money to pay for rent. I think paying rent would be very stressful for some newcomers to Toronto because the day they have rent is like a big deadline for them to see if they have made enough money and didn't buy too much food, and if they do have enough money then it'll just keep going on and on. But then if they don't have enough money they'll be kicked out onto the street then they'll have nowhere to go.

According to another student, upon reflection of their whole experience:

This whole project has taught me how hard it must be for some people to get by each week and every month. It takes a lot of work to prepare a budget and try to stay within it. We should be grateful for what we have because we actually just got lucky. I have realized that I take for granted that I'm not really limited in the choice of foods I get to eat, buying another pair of running shoes that I don't really need, or the amount of times we can go to the movies or to a restaurant.

My mom sometimes says—"You can't have everything you see!" or "You shouldn't have something just because another kid does."—I think that the next time she says one of these things I'll know better what she means.

These are only a couple small examples of how students were powerfully engaged to foster their compassion, caring, and loving-kindness (Miller, 2006). Ultimately, these community service experiences helped foster wonder, joy, and compassion within our class.

THE FUTURE: TO SEW AND TO REAP

Today's Lesson

There is geography within you my child.

It is unique.

Within the caverns of this landscape
dreams sleep.
Some will awaken
others will choose to slumber.
Rejoice in their existence
nurture their vitality,
and work earnestly to bring your dreams to their fruition

—Christopher Russell, N.A

Moving forward as an educator, I will be ever more mindful of the delicate balance between the mind, body, and spirit relationship so that my students may ultimately nurture their soul. I want learning to be a rewarding experience for my students. I want something to be stirred in their head and in their heart... mine as well. Thus, it is vital that I continue to be present, caring, and accountable to my students, their families, and my colleagues in order for holism to have a chance to flourish within and among us (Miller, 2007).

The next step in my evolution as a holistic educator will be to bring contemplation into my classroom. Be it stillness, visualization, walking meditation or some other form of contemplation that agrees with a student, I aspire to help my students pay attention to their inner self so that they may flourish as a young individual and deeply realize their interconnectedness to things: either the geography within them; their childlike sense of wonder; or a landscape's beauty.

EPILOGUE

Whether through the arts, athletics, outdoor education or whatever may help inspire a child; I am now on an irreversible path in terms of teaching and curriculum. During my 17 years in the profession, the most significant moments have come when a deeper connection has been made within and beyond the learning—when the intuitive has been stirred. Now, I'm inspired and prepared to further explore, shape, and negotiate curriculum for my students' inner life.

Like the geography of land, I too am altered by the passing of ages. Thus, my holistic journey continues to unfold. I shall continue to work earnestly to help students bring their dreams to fruition and to ensure that soul, a loving heart, and service are vital parts of my classroom.

REFERENCES

Donahue, D. (1999). Service-learning for preservice teachers: Ethical dilemmas for practice. *Teaching and Teacher Education, 15*, 685–695.

Leggo, C. (2011). Living love: Confessions of a fearful teacher. *Journal of the Canadian Association for Curriculum Studies, 9*(1), 115–144.

Miller, J. P. (2006). *Educating for wisdom and compassion: Creating a climate for timeless learning.* California: Corwin Press.

Miller, J. P. (2007). *The holistic curriculum* (2nd ed.). Toronto: UT Press.

Russell, C. (1993). *A gift from the Orcas.* Unpublished poem.

Russell, C. (1994). *Senility.* Unpublished poem.

Russell, C. (N.A.). *Today's lesson.* Unpublished poem.

CHAPTER 22

DEVELOPING AS A HOLISTIC EDUCATOR

Learning to Understand My Students

Angela Bosco
University of Toronto

I believe that my purpose for teaching is to make children aware of possibilities and to inspire them beyond things that I cannot even imagine, regardless of the difficulties that I may encounter. Miller (2010) agrees with Gandhi's definition of education when he states, "the child includes 'head, hand, and heart'; we could also say body, mind, and spirit," (p. 8). I believe that teachers must consider each child as an individual with needs and strengths when implementing the curriculum and developing teaching strategies.

I've learned several things throughout my career as an educator. I've learned that teaching can be messy and that learning doesn't necessarily happen in a succinct and orderly fashion. I've learned that a holistic program includes different strategies and creative methods of teaching that need to be tailored to the students not to the curriculum. I've learned that flexibility in routines is as important as encouraging children to have

Teaching From the Thinking Heart, pages 195–202

a voice. By getting to know my students I've realized that it is important that they see each other as individuals able to advocate for themselves, and that it is my responsibility to accommodate those individual students. In essence, I've realized that teaching should not be done alone because we are all part of a school community, and as such, only part of a larger learning environment. All that I've learned has brought me to one conclusion: I need always to continue learning.

TEACHING CAN BE MESSY

I can't imagine a class where students sit, day after day, quietly at their desks, working in their notebooks as I lecture away. For the most part, my first administrator saw my way of teaching as ineffective and messy. Her common line was, "How can you be sure they are learning if each one is doing something different?" My grade 4/5/6 class was studying Canada and the provinces. For this unit I had incorporated drama to learn about the physical geography, art to learn about the size and natural resources, and a "facts surprize bag" to learn about all the interesting particulars they could discover about their provinces. I had also asked each student to think of their own activity that might help them learn about Canada. They shared their learning not only with their classmates, but we then decided to share the work with our school. It had been our class's month to decorate the office bulletin board. The children would use the P. A. system each morning to ask the school a question that could only be answered by reading the facts or looking at the three-dimensional maps on the bulletin board.

The results of each day's responses were used in math class to look at things such as the number of correct answers per class, integrating the data into our math program. My principal was bothered that the children worked on language, social studies, math, science, drama, and art activities within the unit about Canada.

I had created in my classroom a situation that González (2001) would agree with in that "...scientific concepts can be transformed into the everyday, into the domain of practice, acquiring meaning and significance, but also enabling conscious reflection and meta-awareness," (p. 28). However, my principal couldn't see how I was going to gauge what the children had learned.

I must have been exceptionally frustrated that day because I asked her to quiz the students on any of the curriculum expectations in the different units. She did. I couldn't have anticipated the level of expertise of the children. The students had not only taken an interest in their own projects, but they had helped each other and so had learned more than I realized. Wilson & Peterson (2006) suggest "learners who understand more about their own learning—researchers call this a *metacognitive awareness*—have greater capacity to transfer their learning to new problems and contexts" (p. 6).

I had prompted my principal out of my own frustration, but that action made me more resolute to continue to teach in an integrated way having seen the excitement the children had in sharing their expertise.

I had used oral quizzes in class before, but I had used them for rote learning exercises and always in such a way that was nonthreatening and voluntary. Although the students took up the challenge, putting them on the spot the way I did with my administrator present, had not been my intention. Over time, I was able to create a holistic program that was both inclusive of different strategies and methods of teaching and also creative so that children were bringing their strengths to their own learning. I realized that the ideal construct is of a teacher who is both student-centered and subject-centered, who is a classroom leader and yet is helping/friendly to students and understanding of their learning needs and problems, a good communicator and able to leave scope for students to develop their own learning potential. (Abbott-Chapman, Hughes, & Williamson, 2001, p. 183).

I'm not sure I can claim to follow the "ideal construct" of a teacher, but as an educator it is important to find ways of integrating the curriculum, so that it becomes meaningful to the students. An integrated approach to teaching opens up possibilities and promotes sharing of diverse abilities among students. Students take part in their own learning and create opportunities for others to learn. My role is not only to complete mandates required by the Ministry of Education, but also to ensure that children are pushing their notions of what is possible and supporting that learning.

TEACHING NEEDS TO BE TAILORED TO THE STUDENTS, NOT TO THE CURRICULUM

I knew that I was teaching well when I saw each student as an individual whom I needed to get to know and understand before I could use the teaching method that would work best for the student. At the beginning of my career, my error was that I didn't understand that success in learning was not only due to teaching methods. Instead, I had captured my students' attention because I could at least see that each one needed to learn in their own way.

Although I always have a vision of how I want the year to progress, and may even have materials and lessons ready to go before the children arrive, I find that they are more a guide than a blueprint. I like to be prepared, "have priorities and focus," but I also understand that being flexible is very important because, "plans end up being contrary to the flow of life and do not allow the principal and teachers to be open to the present moment," so as to also bring the expertise of all the classroom participants into the learning (Miller, 2010, p. 92).

I do set up a very clear routine at the beginning of the year that helps to create consistency and a base from which we all start our day. Although I believe it is important to have a routine, I also find that building in flexibility is also important. Within my morning routine, elements of rote learning usually exist that I feel are necessary because the repeated practice helps to solidify certain skills and makes the rest of the knowledge easier to comprehend, manipulate, and apply. Math and grammar practice are part of all the transitions between activities and between classes so children see that all the time they spend in the classroom is valuable and that they are constantly learning. The classroom environment is very active, but I make up for this by not assigning homework and by allowing for free time every day. I feel that curriculum expectations should never supersede the child's own learning needs. The student is first an individual, and the curriculum, a guide in their learning.

CHILDREN AS INDIVIDUALS WITHIN A GROUP

Discussions and debates happen regularly in my classroom, and I always find ways to encourage children to make themselves heard. The trick has been to find a balance between ensuring a student's own needs are met and having them understand that the class functions as a unit, so each individual's need can only be met if it is not at the expense of someone else's, including the teacher's. It is important that I remember, "Each person owes a debt to others for survival and for the existence of society and should be aware that an injustice done to one person or group of people is an injustice to all human beings," (Miller, 2010, p. 81).

An activity for a unit on ecosystems with my grade four students serves as an example of ensuring that each individual in our class understood the importance of the relationships we shared. Before looking at ecosystems around the world, we dissected how we as a classroom were an ecosystem and how we were all dependent on each other for our learning and for our happiness during that learning. We created an incredible bulletin board of our classroom and included each individual as well as all the necessary elements that ecosystems have in common. Art, language, science were all subjects integrated into this activity. We discussed the behaviors necessary in our classroom ecosystem, guidelines necessary to the very success of such an ecosystem. How we treat and respect each other as individuals became necessary aspects because without respect and responsibility for one's own behavior we would not be able to coexist happily. The grade four class thought about conflict as necessary, and found ways to deal with them so that one person's needs were not going to supersede another's. An atmosphere was created that made classroom management almost unnecessary because I became one of the inhabitants of this system, and we all needed to live in a symbiotic relationship. Each of us was like a species that exists in a different biome. When one organism is threatened it was as if one species fell out of equilibrium within the system; it affected everybody. This isn't to say that classroom management has always been easy or smooth, but rather that I don't take sole responsibility within a classroom. I make sure that each individual understands they are a part of the classroom and responsible for the way the classroom functions.

Differing opinions in groups are important and I encourage children to find their own voice within the class. For years now I have used opinion journals. As the year progresses, children are encouraged to pose the questions they feel should be addressed by their classmates. Sharing of ideas is encouraged throughout the rest of the working periods during the day. I often get an understanding about where the children are in expressing themselves in print, but also where they are as far as language conventions. These journals also help the class to see each other as individuals with feelings and independent thoughts, and also encourage children to find a voice for themselves in a constructive way that doesn't put someone else down. By seeing that, "The whole curriculum is the connected curriculum. The whole curriculum focuses on relationships so that students can make connections," (Miller, 2010, p. 60) children begin to see that their opinions and their views may be different and those differences, just as commonalities, are all part of being a member of a group.

UNDERSTANDING INDIVIDUAL STUDENTS

Getting to know each of my students has been the primary concern in my journey to creating a holistic classroom environment. I begin the year by telling them my own story by showing them a scrapbook that I began in teacher's college filled with important moments in my life because, "Storytelling can be a powerful way of nurturing soul and connecting with students," (Miller, 2007, p. 179). I then ask the children to tell their own stories by creating a similar "all about me scrapbook."

I ask children to bring in favorite photos and keepsakes they can place into this scrapbook and to write about why they want to share such mementoes. Encouraging children to create their own unique scrapbooks with artifacts important to them is a small way I support, " ... an ability to develop students academically, a willingness to nurture and support cultural competence, and the development of a sociopolitical or critical consciousness," (Ladson-Billings, 1995, p. 483).

It is important for teachers to construct meaningful curriculum that takes into consideration that learning is rooted within social events (Scherba de Valenzuela, 2002). We share our scrapbooks in small groups and then include them into our classroom library so that we all get a chance to read each other's books. Over the years, children have taken the concept, changed elements and made it their own. I am always impressed at how hard all the children work on these small visions of themselves and I realize how important it is to be heard within a classroom. It also makes me realize as Miller's (2007) quote of the Dalai Lama so succinctly states that, "compassion for the students' lives or futures not only for their examinations, make your work as a teacher much more effective" (p. 21). Could a writing assessment have given me so much information about each child? I really do believe that to have a truly holistic curriculum the true essential criterions are, "connections and relationships as the main vehicle for realizing the student's true nature" (Miller, The Holistic Curriculum, 2007, p. 178).

TEACHING IS NOT A SOLITARY ENDEAVOR

It is important to see myself as a part of the school community, though early in my teaching career, I often wanted to close my door to conflicting views about how best to teach. Teaching in isolation without the support of colleagues and parents wasn't what I wanted to do; dialogue has been incredibly important in developing my understanding of holistic education and supporting the growth necessary both for myself and my students. Teaching is not, or, at least, should not be a solitary endeavor because learning isn't.

> The psychic rewards and satisfactions of elementary teaching seem, in other words, to come today not just from fleeting and often deferred feedback from individuals, or from success with a few exceptions, but from emotional bonds and emotional understanding established here-and-now with entire groups. (Hargreaves, 2000, p. 818)

When I first began to teach the difficulty lay in creating a holistic program when other teachers were still teaching school subjects in isolation. It was difficult to explain to parents why one teacher was teaching one way while another was doing things differently. There were arguments with teachers that had taught successfully for years and could prove the children were learning after each set of lessons. My teaching, on the other hand, could take weeks, months, or the school year when the culminating activity showed the degree of learning that had taken place.

Through all this, I've learned that it really isn't what and how you teach, because each of those very successful teachers and I had something in common, we cared about our students being successful and happy. I recognized the key factor in common was that we as teachers taught with the children in mind and made changes to our teaching to accommodate our students. I began to experiment with the different strategies that were successful for other teachers. For this reason, I have both transformative culminating activities and rote learning exercise (multiplication and division exercises) that are very much transmission of facts. I've learned that that balance depends on the child rather than the method.

FINAL THOUGHTS

Teaching is messy, and learning doesn't necessarily happen in a succinct and orderly fashion. I do believe that a holistic program includes different strategies, flexibility in routines, and creative methods of teaching, and should be tailored to the students not to the curriculum. I can now appreciate how important it is to encourage children to have a voice and have students advocate for themselves. It is my responsibility to accommodate individual students but it is also my responsibility to be part of a school community of learners. Learning is more than just having the right teaching strategies; it's realizing that understanding our students allows us to incorporate the best teaching strategies.

REFERENCES

Abbott-Chapman, J., Hughes, P., & Williamson, J. (2001). Teachers' perceptions of classroom competencies over a decade of change. *Asian-Pacific Journal of Teacher Education, 29*(2), 171–185.

González, N. (2001). Bridging funds of distributed knowledge: Creating zones of practices in mathematics. *Journal of Education for Students Placed at Risk, 6*(1&2), 115–132.

Hargreaves, A. (2000). Mixed emotions: Teachers' perceptions of their interactions with students. *Teaching and Teacher Education, 16*(8), 811–826.

Ladson-Billings, G. (1995). Towards a theory of culturally relevant pedagogy. *American Educational Research Journal, 32*(3), 465–491.

Miller, J. P. (2007). *The holistic curriculum.* Toronto: University of Toronto Press.

Miller, J. P. (2010). *Whole child education.* Toronto: University of Toronto Press Incorporated.

Rowe, K. (2004). The importance of teaching:Ensuring better schooling by building teacher capacities that maximize the quality of teaching and learning provision—implications of findings from theinternational and Australian evidence-based research. *Making Schools Better Conference: A Summit Conference on the Performance, Management and Funding of Australian Schools.* Australian Council for Educational Research (ACER).

Scherba de Valenzuela, J. (2002, July). *Sociocultural theory.* Retrieved July 12, 2011, from Julia Scherba de Valenzuela, Ph.D.: http://www.unm.edu/~devalenz/handouts/sociocult.html

Seidl, B. (2007). Working with communities to explore and personalize culturally relevant pedagogy: "Push, double images, and double talk." *Journal of Teacher Education, 58*(2), 168–183.

Wilson, S. M., & Peterson, P. L. (2006). *Theories of learning and teaching: What do they mean for educators? Working Paper.* Washington, DC: National Education Association Research Department.

CHAPTER 23

TEACHING IS A WILD RIDE

Melanie van de Water
University of Toronto

Nobody actually says they want to be a teacher. When you ask a child what they want to be when they grow up, you get lofty answers: brain surgeon, firefighter, but never a teacher. How could I say I wanted to be a teacher? How could I ever want to be something so average? I eventually realized that I had to be honest with myself. I knew teens. I loved books. And so I became a high school English teacher.

How ordinary.

There are some days I would give my right arm to be able to hide behind a computer, to be able to waltz into the office, latte in hand, sit down, and leisurely check my inbox. Instead, the elaborate song and dance required of a classroom teacher, day after day, is difficult. If you have ever stood in front of adolescents you have had the experience of being at the helm of the world's most critical audience. Making learning fun is tough. You try to excite your students you say, "So, guys, we're starting *Othello* today!" They look at you, dubiously. If I could go back in time though, I would tell my younger self that there is no better job than being a teacher. I would tell myself that the material is secondary. What matters to students is that you care

Teaching From the Thinking Heart, pages 203–206
Copyright © 2014 by Information Age Publishing
All rights of reproduction in any form reserved.

about them and that you want them to succeed, not only in your course, but in life. I would tell myself that there is no better job in the world.

If you ask a teacher to recall their first day teaching they will grimace like they have just been required to divulge a most unpleasant memory. I have tried to put that day into my mental trash box, but to no avail. I stood in front of my class and panicked. I worried that my skirt was too short. Did they think I was ugly? Or worse, old? (I was twenty-three). Were my clothes cool enough? Was I trying to be "too cool"? I delivered a PowerPoint lecture sitting down and watched my students lose interest. One kid took out his phone. One student asked to go to the bathroom. Several gazed out the window, their heads slumped in their hands. One kid flipped open his laptop. His buddy snickered at something online. Then, mercifully, it was over. I asked if there were any questions. Laptop Boy asked if they were allowed to go. And he called me "Miss." I went home and cried.

The classroom is a different place from when I was a student. It has taken me a while to get used to the technology that is omnipresent in my students' lives. The discipline issues I deal with are related to the Internet. I discovered grade 9 students who, on a school trip, lit themselves on fire and posted it on Facebook. I have suspended a student for creating a false profile of a classmate and posting it on a dating website. I have had a phone call from United States security informing our school that a student was making threatening remarks on an Obama website at that exact moment, and asking us to deal with the student accordingly.

Teachers are never free from the eye of their students. One morning, one of my students asked how I liked the Maple Leafs game the night before. I looked at him quizzically, "Were you there?" He smiled and took out his phone. "No," he said, "but you were." Taking the phone from his hand, I looked at the image. It was a picture of me at the game, 20-ounce beer in hand, Maple Leafs scoreboard in the background. Underneath was a caption with an emoticon of a beer mug, "Work period in Ms. Vdw's class tomorrow?!" I was super vigilant in class that day. I was especially articulate describing Shakespeare's Sonnet 112, and assigned extra homework, feeling like a teenager who had been caught out after curfew.

As a teacher, you are a minor celebrity, and your fans are everywhere. There are times when you can expect to run into your students. I do not go to shopping malls on a Saturday. I rarely attend the movies. I carefully survey the crowd at sporting events. Celebrities are sometimes caught off guard though, such as the time I was spotted on the subway enroute to a bachelorette party dressed as a sexy devil.

Even worse are the times when you are so completely blindsided that as much as you try to summon up your teacher persona and your authoritative demeanor, you are simply unprepared. One winter, I was coming out of a bar in a nearby ski town, with a group of friends. It was last call, closing time, when the group of us spilled out into the street. I was laughing, winding up to throw a snowball in a fastball-type maneuver at my brother when I heard a young, just-broken voice yell. "Hey! It's Ms. van de Water!"

There are certain times when hearing the "Ms." in front of your name makes your heart drop. Fitting rooms are one of them. Ditto for having your eyebrows waxed, hair cut, or anything involving personal care. The LCBO is awkward, but nothing prepares you for hearing your teacher name at two-o-clock in the morning leaving a bar.

I dropped the snowball as three youths ran up to me, open beers in hand. "We knew it was you! Look! We're drinking!" they shouted, waving open bottles of Molson Canadian in my face. "You can't suspend us! We're not in school!" They cackled and howled, falling over themselves. I looked blankly at them. My husband pulled up the fur hood on my ski jacket. I heard my brother's voice in my ear, "Just walk away." I pulled my hood even tighter around my head and marched into the blinding snow, as the boys pursued me, hounding me like the paparazzi. I headed toward the ring of taxicabs, praying I would not have to wait in the taxi circle with my three drunk students. I expected some fallout from this late-night teacher spotting the following Monday at school, but the boys could not look me in the eye for the rest of the year.

There should be a travel manual for every teacher-to-be. A chapter in it might be called "Oh, The Places You'll Go," as a nod to Dr. Seuss. In my years as a teacher, I have travelled to Boston, Washington, Pittsburg, France, Italy, and Germany. I have spent weeks at summer camps and re-treats all over the province. I have spent three days hauling canoes through the swampy, buggy forest and sleeping in a tent with my colleagues and a German tripper. I took 14 students on a service trip to the Caribbean build-ing schools in the interior of the Dominican Republic. We slept in mos-quito nets. I asked my students to draw me a smiley face each morning to convey how their bowels were each day. On a trip to Europe we spent a day tramping around museums in Florence. A student had blisters so inflamed, I spent the evening inserting a sterilized needle into her feet, popping red, water-filled blisters. I had three students caught by the police for drinking at a Pittsburg Pirates game. We flew them home at their parents' expense.

While illness and discipline issues are par for the course, I have experi-enced my most wonderful teaching moments on these trips. I stood in awe at the foot of the Statue of David with my grade 11 students. A student, so touched by a 9/11 story, sat on the floor of the Pentagon and cried. I painted a schoolhouse wall in the heat of the interior Dominican Republic listening to my student tell me the details about her grueling experiences as a com-petitive gymnast. I spent the day snowboarding with a group of boys in their graduating year while they chanted, "Do it!" from the bottom of a jump.

There are times when you must tread lightly on the line between teach-er and student. During a winter camping trip I slept in an ice igloo with four of my 15-year old students. This experience prepared me to survive my own daughter's adolescence. When young girls ask questions about sex, drugs, and cliques it is akin to the little Dutch boy pulling his finger out of the dam. A torrent is unleashed, and there is no question that remains unasked once they know you have answers. The following morning, I was nervous. Did I give too much information? Although I had tried to keep my teacher persona throughout our discussion, I got a little delirious by midnight in the confined space and frigid temperature. I ran into one of these girls, years later. That night, she said, was one of her best memories of high school. She told me that when asked to write about a good teacher, she had written about me. Flattered, I smiled, knowing that my analysis of Holden's demise in *The Catcher in the Rye* was likely not included in her prose about good teaching.

A teacher's job is to impart moral knowledge. Over the years, I have had my students write thank-you notes for plays, performances, and museum tours. I have reminded them to thank their parents for the drum lessons, math tutor, or iPhone. I have tried to instill academic honesty. I confronted one of my students about four paragraphs in his final paper taken from the Internet. He confessed to handing in his older sister's essay. His older sister had been in my class two years earlier and had received an "A" on the same paper. Plagiarism included.

From time to time, I see some of my former students. Something akin to a truth serum must have been dispensed at graduation because they feel compelled to confess their sins. Danielle told me that the reason they lost the volleyball tournament in Kingston was because they had sneaked out to drink tequila. John admitted he never actually read the book for his book report. Joey told me that even though he plagiarized his final essay, he still thought my class was cool. They say other things, too. Emily told me that she read *The Pillars of the Earth*, all 1,000 pages because I said it was my favorite book. James told me he had never received an "A" on anything until he took my class. Katie said she went to teacher's college because I always talked about how wonderful being a teacher is. Justin said he was really sorry for being such a shit.

Being a teacher is not glamorous. There are no fancy trips, expense accounts, or client dinners. But looking back on the decision I made as a young adult, I am proud of the courage it took to do something I perceived as ordinary. I know what it is like to be a high school student. As an adult, I try to offer wisdom and support to help get them through their adolescence. Every day, I am thankful that I touch lives, however briefly. I have a box full of cards, letters, and messages, which I look at often. I am happy I do not sell ad space for potato chips, or work in a bank. Teachers who inspire me have taught me that to teach is to take risks every day. I felt I was a much better teacher before I had students, but I know having students has made me a much better person. Someday I'll tell them how much they have taught me.

CHAPTER 24

THE THINKING HEART

The Editors

THE THINKING HEART: FINAL REFLECTIONS

From the beginning it was our intent to glean authentic descriptions that directly address how teachers allow the thinking heart space and time within their classroom. It was not necessarily our aim to develop a new conceptual framework for wisdom and compassion, but rather to understand more fully how holistic education's key concepts are relatable to a diverse range of educational settings.

The book reads as an embodied example of holistic teaching and learning and presents as a guide for teachers who wish to affirm and expand their curriculum practices as well as reflect on who they are becoming as educators. We learned through working with the experiences of these teachers that the opportunity to voice from within what is already known to be true about teaching holistically is more the beginning point for a foreseeable change in education than developing new frameworks.

When Jack Miller read the original class papers there was a sense that ideas resonant with holism were already present in the thoughts and lives of these teachers. They were not reaching, grasping for, or developing arguments to please the professor. They were writing from their core, from within a passion and love truly held for the act of teaching and learning. In keeping with the thinking heart's way of knowing, the writing process was

Teaching From the Thinking Heart, pages 207–212
Copyright © 2014 by Information Age Publishing

one of resonation—that subtle, yet tangible internal feeling that appears slowly, at times flows easily, at others, awkwardly, but is still supported by the sentiment, "I know this, I do this, I want to voice it in words so that the reader will understand." All the while it seems as if this subtle awareness is connected to a love that dares not speak its name when standardized testing becomes the ultimate litmus test for successful learning.

We suggest that the beauty of these papers is their specificity and connection to the life of the classroom as well as the life experiences of these teachers. In reading and editing these papers we identified four themes. These include the whole student, inner authority, authenticity, and community. Given the number of contributions and the diversity of perspectives presented, we recognize that individuals may find other themes that arise as they read these papers. To abstract themes then involves the risk that so much of this experience will be dismissed. Still, we think it is worth looking for transcendent ideas that run throughout this book.

THE WHOLE STUDENT

Teaching with the whole student in mind requires concrete curriculum and pedagogical approaches. Students are brought to life in these chapters in the spirit of Ghandi's commitment to the simultaneous engagement of the head, the heart, and the hands during learning. Students also possess distinct ontologies, races, and cultural identities, and yet these distinct identities can, even in a moment of honored difference, harmonize with the class as a whole. We also learn that when teachers commit to students as whole beings, feelings, emotions, curiosities, and intelligences are nourished together through integrated pedagogies.

Transdisciplinary learning is already an expressed goal in mainstream public schooling, but it has not become a widespread curriculum practice. Ryder, Forsythe, and Bosco are educational forerunners as they show how students can learn effectively when subjects are gathered together under one broad theme. Motivated by a concern that curriculum expectations would not be fulfilled, Bosco's school principal visited her class to test the students on their knowledge. The quiz results revealed that the class acquired an in-depth grasp on curriculum expectations.

Teachers who introduce diverse curriculum perspectives see time and classroom management in a way that trusts the organic unfolding of experience as opposed to constantly pushing towards particular outcomes. Ryder notes that a classroom engaged in either transformative or transdisciplinary learning may initially appear chaotic and less productive, but inquiry based learning protects the students' capacity to wonder and to question. Aglipay and Forsythe point out that time becomes elastic; it can breathe with the human needs of students.

Many of these public and private school teachers were insistent on the notion that the presence of soul leads to meaningful and vital learning. Donohue outlines her approach to soulful physical education. To ensure the authentic presence of soul in the writing, the teachers were asked: what do you really mean by this notion of soul? If the teacher provided an in-depth meaning and a thick description of practice, the reference to soul remained. We learned that words like soul are as problematic as any other word that attempts to capture what it means to think and learn, and therefore we believe that soul deserves a presence in educational discourse, a chance to be explored and further articulated. Parker Palmer (2004) argues that many learning spaces already affirm the intellect, emotions, and will, but "we know very little about creating spaces that invite the soul to make itself known . . . —and we seem to place little value on preserving the soul spaces in nature" (p. 56).

AUTHENTICITY

To be authentic means to remain faithful to interior ideals despite pressures from the external world. An existentialist view suggests conforming to external expectations inhibits authenticity. This is the tension that meets teachers daily. The teacher stories within these pages either explicitly or implicitly address this pressure, but all do address it.

Not only do we need to define our true self, we need to defend our authenticity to facilitate a holistic classroom. And in these pages, we have witnessed teachers unabashedly considering not only the necessity, but the costs of presenting their real selves in the classroom. Nina Moore does this in her "Dearest Students" letter as she addresses her students and considers what they have taught her. Elana Freeman attends to authenticity as she considers the benefits of a deep honesty between student and teacher. Melanie van de Water rejoices in her relationships with her students, willing to make mistakes and learn alongside them, using her personality and instinct as her primary means of connection. Grant Minkhorst implies authenticity as he presents his optimistic "Happiness Project" that meets opposition in his teaching context. These and the other teachers are taking an Aristotelian view of authenticity as a creative act, an act of virtue that is cultivated through honesty and thought.

It is a constant struggle, being in relation to the world, to be true to oneself despite restrictions. As teachers, we enter the classroom with the weight of expectation to balance the internal and the external. These teacher stories acknowledge the tension, but encourage us to push through to authenticity.

INNER AUTHORITY

In their original form, many of the essays in this text were titled *My Journey*. This was a most apt decision by the authors because they were trying to get to the heart of their teaching experience. They knew their struggle was important, their experience was important, and what they were describing was a development of ideas, principles, and beliefs. So, at its heart, this book is about teachers making sense of what they do, what works and what doesn't, who believes in their work and who doesn't. It is an examination of not only what they do, but who they become as they do it.

And so we struggled and debated about what to name this becoming by way of the teaching journey. It was in the process of editing the essays that the teachers gained clarity, or so it seems from the seat of an editor. We asked the authors to name the "aboutness" of their journey, and what they most wanted to discover and share. Some came to clarity quickly, that their work was about overcoming reductionist opposition in order to teach holistically, or about community building in the ESL classroom, or about a specific pedagogy that excited them and engaged their students. Other authors struggled to find the strongest defining factor of their teaching experience to date. But what all authors were engaged in was discovering their authority.

As Parker Palmer (1998) suggests, "Authority comes as I reclaim my identity and integrity, remembering my selfhood and my sense of vocation" (p. 33). In these pages, the work of reclaiming identity and integrity has been revealed, and what we sense is a coming to power sourced from within. Inner authorities are earned by an unwillingness to follow scripts (Palmer, 1998, p. 33) and expectations, and create meaning from inner lives and lived experience. The teachers in these pages have authored their own becoming. Palmer continues, "Then teaching can come from the depths of my own truth—and the truth that is within my students a chance to respond in kind." To author the teaching and learning experience, to teach from true authority sourced from the heart, has enabled these educators to journey from an ideal to a practical commitment, and they encourage us to do the same.

COMMUNITY

Reconciling educational ideals with the reality of what presents itself, authentic embodiment and understanding students as whole human beings, directly plays into what it means to treat the classroom as a community. These concluding thoughts were discussed at the time that an article with a disturbing message appeared in the local city paper; our social spaces are "swimming in a culture of mean" (Menon, 2013). If the archetypal bully is showing up in on-line communications, the workplace, and our cultural spaces, what can we realistically expect of the classroom? Although these pages do not offer a panacea for eradicating meanness, we do note that teachers who are committed to soulful learning also feel that a safe and harmonious classroom community has to be consciously fostered. Lowes makes this simple point when she writes that teachers should practice what they wish to see in society, within their classroom.

Practices that foster a caring learning community are introduced herein; breathing together, sharing in circles, service-learning, group mandalas, meditation, mindfulness, and finally simply being in nature together. All of these activities access the root of human existence and thus provide the atmosphere for fundamental connection. As Aglipay points out, our lives are based on the principle of interconnectedness, and when teachers focus on the experience of connection, classroom learning and relationships are enhanced together.

A holistic classroom is not a compilation of thirty closed subjects. Honoring the recent passing of Nelson Mandela and affirming Charles' reference to *ubuntu*, we offer the words of Archbishop Desmond Tutu (1999). Ubuntu

> . . . speaks of the very essence of being human. It is to say "Hey, so-and-so has ubuntu." Then you are generous, you are hospitable, you are friendly and caring and compassionate. You share what you have. It is to say, "My humanity is caught up, is inextricably bound up, in yours." We belong in a bundle of life. We say, "A person is a person through other persons." (p. 31)

Our humanity, as it is bound up in the other, cannot be felt while feeling defensive or guarded. In fact, what it means to be human together is more easily accessed through shared vulnerability. Charles and Verhaeghe introduce strategies that help students to drop their guard. Warmth and openness in language learning are vitally important. Freeman also supports this point in relation to having difficult discussions about race and politics in her language-learning classroom. The courage to acknowledge power relations, something that we believe is extremely necessary and important for equitable learning, should not come at the expense of knowing what to do to cultivate a student's sense of belonging. Complex power dynamics and the deep sensitivity to connect with others can exist in balance.

Finally, we believe the teachers in this book work from what Palmer calls the "undivided self." Palmer (1998) writes, "In the undivided self every major thread of one's life experience is honored, creating a weave of such coherence and strength that it can hold students and subjects as well as self" (p. 15). The papers here reveal that "coherence and strength." These teachers have each developed their own voice which reflects an integrated and undivided self. We believe these voices can inspire other teachers as they navigate the challenges of the classroom to connect with head, hands, and hearts of their students.

REFERENCES

Menon, V. (2013). Mean: We are living in an age of nastiness, deceit, and malice. *Toronto Star.* (IN2-IN5)

Palmer, P. (2004). *A hidden wholeness: The journey toward an undivided life.* San Francisco: Jossey-Bass.

Palmer, P. (1998). *The courage to teach.* San:Francisco: Jossey-Bass Publishers.

Tutu, D. (1999). *No future without forgiveness.* New York: Doubleday.

ABOUT THE EDITORS

Michèle Irwin earned her MFA in Writing at Vermont College, and is currently finishing a doctorate at the University of Toronto. She has presented papers internationally on writing process and pedagogy. She is at work on a Middle Grade series and a novel.

John (Jack) Miller has been working in the field of holistic education for over 35 years. He is author/editor of 18 books on holistic learning and contemplative practices in education which include, *The Contemplative Practitioner, Education and the Soul, The Holistic Curriculum,* and *Educating for Wisdom and Compassion.* His writing has been translated into nine languages. Jack has worked extensively with holistic educators in Hong Kong, Japan, and Korea, and has been a visiting professor at two universities in Japan. Jack teaches courses on holistic education and spirituality in education at the Ontario Institute for Studies in Education at the University of Toronto where he is Professor.

Kelli Nigh is a professional singer and actor who developed a unique approach to mind–body inquiry in the drama classroom. This approach was introduced to students in a diverse range of educational settings, including community arts centers, and public and private schools. Kelli recently completed her doctoral research at the Ontario Institute for Studies in Education, University of Toronto. She has taught holistic education and human development courses in teacher education programs and looks forward to further pursuing her research interests in ecology, youth, and embodied learning.

ABOUT THE CONTRIBUTORS

Stephanie Aglipay is currently pursuing her MA in Curriculum, Teaching and Learning as a part-time student at OISE. Her interests in education include conflict resolution programs, community and school relations, and high-needs schools. She has recently started her teaching career and is working full-time in a Toronto elementary school.

Angela Bosco is currently a primary/junior educator with the Toronto District School Board in Toronto, Canada. She is also a PhD Student at the Ontario Institute of Studies in Education at the University of Toronto. Her research interests include exploring methods of teaching that enhance academic success focusing on the whole child as an individual.

Merlin Charles is a teacher educator at OISE, University of Toronto, as well as a post-secondary French as a second language (FSL) instructor. Merlin is interested in cultivating teaching presence through holistic, communicative, and innovative approaches to language teaching and learning, in all contexts.

Peggy Donohue is passionate about sport, physical activity, fitness, and well-being. She teaches Health and Physical Education in the junior, intermediate, and senior levels at a Toronto independent school. Peggy holds a BEd in Physical Education from McGill University and an MEd in Curriculum, Teaching and Learning from the Ontario Institute for Studies in Education. She believes that a positive and meaningful experience in

Teaching From the Thinking Heart, pages 215–219
Copyright © 2014 by Information Age Publishing

Phys. Ed. can inspire students to lead healthy and active lives long after they have left "gym class."

Ximena Barría Fernández is a teacher of deaf students from Chile and has been working in the field since 1995. In 1999, she launched a school for the deaf in collaboration with other colleagues. Ximena obtained her Bachelor degree at UMCE in 1999 and obtained a master's degree from the Ontario Institute of Studies in Education last June 2013.

Jennifer Forsythe graduated with a degree in Early Childhood Education from Ryerson University in 1998 and recently completed her Master of Education in 2012 from the University of Toronto. Throughout her teaching career, Jennifer has held a variety of teaching positions in an inner city school in Toronto. Currently, Jennifer is teaching grade 4/5 and is actively involved in a number of leadership roles within her school setting. Jennifer has always been very passionate about teaching and is an advocate of holistic education in public schools.

Elana Freeman has been teaching adult English language learners for the past seven years. She has a Bachelor of Fine Arts from Concordia University and a Masters in Second Language Education from the Ontario Institute for Studies in Education at the University of Toronto.

Dan Gullery first started teaching in Montreal, where he worked for three years as a high school English teacher. In 2012, Dan moved with his partner to Toronto to pursue a Masters of Education degree from OISE at the University of Toronto. He plans to continue to find ways to bridge his love for teaching and cooking.

Michèle Irwin earned her MFA in Writing at Vermont College, and is currently finishing a doctorate at the University of Toronto. She has presented papers internationally on writing process and pedagogy. She is at work on a Middle Grade series and a novel.

Ahmed Kandil is a PhD candidate at the University of Toronto. Throughout his educational career, which started in 1992, Mr. Kandil played the roles of TESOL instructor, curriculum designer, instructional supervisor, teacher trainer, and unit coordinator. His main research interests are related to instructional supervision and the teaching of vocabulary.

Nyambura Isabell Kariuki, a grade four teacher, was born in Nairobi, Kenya and moved away as a young child to the United States. She has lived in Canada for the past 20 years and has been an elementary teacher for the last ten. Nyambura recently completed a Masters of Education in Curriculum Studies and Teacher Development. In her spare time she loves reading, watching movies, and travelling to different places around the world.

Maria Karmiris is a teacher with the TDSB (Toronto District School Board). She has been teaching elementary students for twelve years (K-6). She just recently completed her Masters of Education at OISE (Ontario Institure for Studies in Education). She is currently teaching students with special needs. She believes that learning is a life long process, which involves being supported by and supporting others along their respective journeys.

Sarah Lowes is a graduate of OISE's M.Ed Curriculum Studies and Teacher Development program with a specialization in Environmental Education. She has studied education since 2006, and teaches at the elementary level in Halton. Sarah maintains an active public profile online as a writer for *TheRookieTeacher.ca* and as the publisher of *Alternative Times*, a weekly online newspaper focused on topics in Environmental Education and Sustainability.

John (Jack) Miller has been working in the field of holistic education for over 35 years. He is author/editor of 18 books on holistic learning and contemplative practices in education which include, *The Contemplative Practitioner, Education and the Soul, The Holistic Curriculum*, and *Educating for Wisdom and Compassion*. His writing has been translated into nine languages. Jack has worked extensively with holistic educators in Hong Kong, Japan, and Korea, and has been a visiting professor at two universities in Japan. Jack teaches courses on holistic education and spirituality in education at the Ontario Institute for Studies in Education at the University of Toronto where he is Professor.

Grant Minkhorst is an elementary school teacher with the Halton District School Board. With nine years as a classroom teacher, Grant has spent most of his time teaching in the Intermediate division. He is active in a number of areas with the school board, including the New Teacher Induction Program (NTIP) steering committee as well as serving as an associate teacher for new teacher candidates. While completing his Master of Education at the Ontario Institute of Education (University of Toronto), Grant focused his research on teacher education reform and student engagement.

Nina Moore is an elementary educator with the TDSB and has been teaching for 12 years. Practicing holistic education has enabled her to counter a culture of standardization and outcome-orientated schooling.

Jill Morris is a secondary teacher with the Toronto District School Board. She loves her work and every day appreciates how fortunate she is to be working with such marvelous young people.

Kelli Nigh is a professional singer and actor who developed a unique approach to mind–body inquiry in the drama classroom. This approach was introduced to students in a diverse range of educational settings, including community arts centers, and public and private schools. Kelli recently completed her doctoral research at the Ontario Institute for Studies in Education, University of Toronto. She has taught holistic education and human development courses in teacher education programs and looks forward to further pursuing her research interests in ecology, youth, and embodied learning.

Chris Russell has taught and coached students in Grades 1–6, and been a Strategic Program Leader for Inquiry during his 18-year career as an educator. In addition to his current teaching role, he is also a part-time MEd student at OISE. One day, Christopher hopes to work with teachers in training or become involved in the development and implementation of educational policy.

Rebecca Ryder, as a mom, a student, a coach, and an educator, believes strongly in approaching teaching and learning experiences holistically and through the lens of inquiry. Rebecca graduated with an Honors BA from Queen's University and studied primary education at the University of Strathclyde in Scotland. Rebecca taught overseas in international schools for many years and currently teaches at Upper Canada College, an IB World School, in Toronto.

Melanie van de Water has been in the teaching profession for over ten years, mostly in the independent school system. As a teacher of English and Social Science, Melanie enjoys her classes best when they go off track. Her philosophy on education is to teach from the heart and always tries her best to put herself in her students' shoes.

Julia Verhaeghe has taught ESL in Thailand, India, and Canada over the past three years. She is currently teaching in Toronto at George Brown College. What drew Julia to teaching is what holds her there—building connections with students and learning their stories.

Melanie Viglas is currently a candidate for the Doctor of Philosophy program in the department of Applied Psychology and Human Development at the Ontario Institute for Studies in Education, University of Toronto.

She is a registered Early Childhood Educator and a certified teacher with the Ontario College of Teachers. After teaching kindergarten for five years, she returned to OISE to pursue her doctoral studies in the PhD Early Learning Cohort program. Her research study involved implementing an age-appropriate mindfulness-based program in kindergarten classrooms to explore its impact on young children's self-regulation and prosocial behavior.

INDEX

CPSIA information can be obtained at www.ICGtesting.com
Printed in the USA
LVOW04s0044260914

405958LV00002B/3/P